A FULL LIFE
IN DITCHLING, HASSOCKS AND
BURGESS HILL
1919 – 1997

John Stenning when he won the prize baby competition. From 'The Beacon'
a weekly news-sheet for Ditchling & District, Friday 17th September, 1920

A FULL LIFE
IN DITCHLING, HASSOCKS AND BURGESS HILL
1919 – 1997

by
JOHN STENNING

COUNTRY BOOKS

Published and distributed by:
Country Books
Courtyard Cottage, Little Longstone, Bakewell, Derbyshire DE45 1NN
for:
John Stenning
13 South View, Ditchling, Hassocks, West Sussex BN6 8TQ

ISBN 1 898941 10 6

Cover pictures:
Front:
John Stenning – the prize winning baby competition 1920
Main picture:
Anne of Cleves House, Ditchling
Back cover:
John Stenning, David Cragg and Len Jarrett in The Sandrock August 1985
Photo courtesy of Ptof John V Lord, Ditchling

Acknowledgements:
Thanks to Professor John V Lord; Gertie Thornton; John Mott, photogrpaher; grandchildren Rachel and Andrew; and my wife, Anastasia, who gave me so much help and
encouragement to write this book and paint with watercolours at 77 years of age.

Design and Production by: Dick Richardson, Country Books
Little Longstone, Derbyshire DE45 1NN

Printed and bound in England by:
MFP Design & Print, Stretford, Manchester M32 0JT

Foreword

Twenty-five years ago I recall coming across a man, with a shock of white wavy hair, busily tending his allotment. The scene was rather like the photograph of him on page 22. His burgeoning vegetable plot was situated just by the entrance gate near the water pump on the eastern side of North End Lane in Ditchling, Sussex. Somehow he had managed to win the battle of getting rid of the rampant crop of mare's tail which has always persisted in growing in these allotments. This pernicious weed even manages to grow through the pavements of the Dumbrell's estate hereabouts. I later met him in the local pubs where we would have a chat over a pint of ale during games of darts and bar billiards. He was a man whose eyes always seemed to be glistening with smiles. His name was John Stenning.

He used to enchant me with his tales about life in Ditchling in the old days when the village High Street was bustling with shops, at a time when cars and lorries were seldom seen. Testimony of those tranquil village streets, where children once played safely, can be seen in the photographs which are included in the book. In those days it was the sound of trotting horses that could be heard. Now it is the perpetual rumble of traffic and the stink of car exhausts that we have to endure if we venture into the High Street. In a 1960s photograph on page 28 we can see Len Jarrett, with one of farmer Widdicombe's daughters, driving the Court Gardens Farm sheep through the village Higll Street; probably the last time a flock was driven through the village.

The village of Ditchling lies below the southem slopes of the South Downs, at their highest point, and is about eight miles north of Brighton. It has a population of some 1,760 people. It is a diverse and well integrated community which has many clubs and which organises many social events. A once rural community has now chanlged largely to one of commuters. Quite a number of farms have ceased working in recent years and not long ago the North Star pub, where I first met John, closed down. Court Gardens Farm, at the north-west end of the village where John worked for a number of years as a young man, is still active. It is currently a 180 acre farm in all, with a flock of 5()() ewes and 5() acres of arable land, growing mainly wheat and peas. Somewhere, near one of the outbuildings, is the vestigial remains of John's old cauavan inl which he lived as a farm lad before the war

Walking down Ditchling High Street on a Fair Day, when the stalls are set out and the colourful bunting is flapping above our heads, is a treat indeed. The traffic is banned from driving through the street all morning for the festivities, a time when villagers gather together to chat with each other; to buy a plant, a home-made cake or a second-hand book; to munch upon a bacon sandwich for breakfast; to see people in fancy dress; to listen to the Maystons' barrel organ or the ringing of the hand-bells; and to hear the vicar's proclamation of the Fair Queen, with his amusing reference to the village inmates, who are called – 'ye saucy coxcombs, ye doddipol jolt-heads, ye jobbernol goosecaps, ye noddy meacocks, ye flutch calf lollies and ye slapsauce fellows'. It is a village of great characters and personalities, too numerous to mention here except to say that John Stenning is certainly one of them.

I have always been interested in reading how village folk of all occupations have lived their lives in times gone by, particularly when they have described it for themselves. In this way we are able to obtain a reliable pictule of how people really lived and if they set their memories down they can ultimately become valuable social documents. We ate able to capture a more vivid pictute about every day life in a village when it is told by a villager *at first hand* rather than through the second-hand siftings of a professional historian. During our conversations I would often encourage John to write down anecdotes about his life before they evaporated from his memory. Sadly, in recent years, he has been confined to his home in South View, looked after by Ann, his wonderful wife of 55 years marriage. But gladly he has spent his time fruitfully in preparing and bringing to life this delightful memoir of events. He has also included a selection of splendid old photographs of the Ditchling area which have come from his own and his nephew Michael Alford's collections.

John Stenning has lived a rich and varied life – from chemist's and butcher's delivery boy to milkman and cow hand. He has done just about every job there is to do on a farm. He has worked as a thatcher, a 'thistle-dodger', a cleaner of beagling shoes, as well as 'running the drag' for the hunt. He was an armourer with the RAF during the 1939-45 war and after the age of fifty he took up the occupation of nurse. What is more – he has been ball boy at a tennis club a versatile sportsman, an enthusiastic gardener and a family man. He was once even a church choir singer, as a young lad, before he got expelled for lobbing a rotten potato at a choir mistress's dress!

This is an engaging life of a robust and enthusiastic man who has written spontaneously from the heart. He has taken us back in time to a world of rural England when people in the country somehow managed to scratch a living, working at whatever was at hand. You had to be willing to develop new skills quickly. You had to be versatile and take on anything that was available at any one time and John took everything on as a fresh challenge and with an optimistic spirit.

Both happy and sad moments jostle together in his compelling narrative. We learn about his fear of walking alone in the darkness of the 'Keymer Straight' and his signing of the pledge, which he was soon to break! He watched people playing cricket among the cow pats and he kicked a football on a pitch where sheep got trapped in goal-post nets. Once (as a butcher's delivery boy in a hurry to play in a game of cricket) he hid by a hedge and cut the fat from a portion of steak with his penknife to appease the fussy recipients, thus saving himself the journey of going back to the shop. Here we can relive the vivid atmosphere of the times in which John Stenning has lived – a warmly human account of a life lived to the full, 'a full life' indeed.

John Vernon Lord

20/10/97

A FULL LIFE
in Ditchling, Hassocks and Burgess Hill
1919 – 1997

My father moved to Bulls Barn Farm early in the 1900's. He was a harness-maker by trade, doing part of his training at Hurstpierpoint and the remainder at Ditchling. He was a good runner, retaining the ten miles champion of Sussex for three years. He also represented Brighton and County Harriers in the South of Thames race and received a medal for completing the course within a certain time.

He took over the running of the farm, where my brother Gordon and sisters Doris, Vena and Iris were born. Bulls Barn bungalow was a construction of wood and corrugated tin and was often referred to as the 'Tin Bungalow'.

My father married three times, having two children by his first wife, four by the second and two by the third. People who knew him said he was always a very hard working man. In the early days he carried his milk twice a day on yokes to Burgess Hill, then later he used a pony and trap. He also used the yokes to water the animals.

He principally trained for his running on the Common and local roads. Whilst he did road running he was accompanied by Mr Bateup, who cycled alongside him to help him keep his pace. After they had run a good ten miles on the road, my father would finish off running around the perimeter of the Common. He often jogged to meetings at the Dripping Pan in Lewes and sometimes to Brighton and Haywards Heath to compete.

His father was a Farm Bailiff who had eight boys and one girl. His children had a good upbringing. All the brothers did quite well in life going in for various trades. The eldest brother Frederick Penfold was a Dragoon Guard. He was killed at the battle of Abu Klea in 1885 at the age of twenty two. The youngest brother, Hartley won the distinguished service medal for

Fathers family taken at Twineham

The young family at Gospels

In Affectionate Remembrance

OF

FREDERICK PENFOLD STENNING,

(2nd Dragoon Guards),

BORN AUGUST 13TH, 1862,

KILLED AT THE BATTLE OF ABU KLEA, JANUARY 17TH, 1885,

AGED 22 YEARS.

" *The Lord giveth, and the Lord taketh away ;*
Blessed be the name of the Lord."

Fathers eldest brother

Father with cats and caravan
(lived in by Val Kilbride)

Yokes used by father at
Ditchling Common in the early
1900s.
They contained two x four gallons
and weighed 80lbs.

10

Bulls Barn Bungalow, Ditchling Common drawn by Andrew Stenning

The Friars Oak Guest House, Hassocks. The lady in the centre is my mother

gallantry in the first world war. It could be said that the most successful was Frank, who with Mr Green, started the Greens sponge mixture and custard powder business which is still going today. My uncle and Mr Green were firstly partners in a small grocers shop which they closed when the custard powder and sponge mixture business took off. The remaining brothers also had successful careers. Three that spring to mind are a Headmaster, an

11

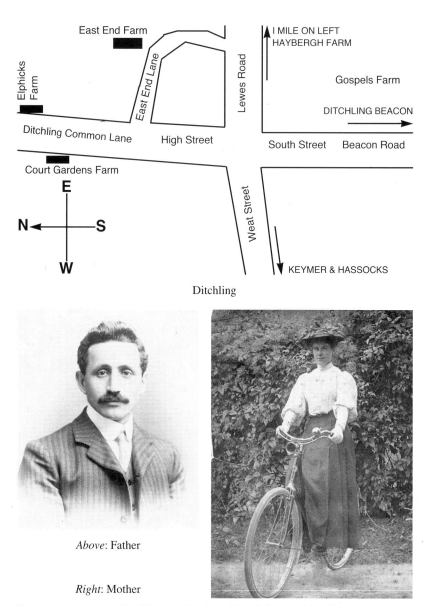

East End Farm

East End Lane

Elphicks Farm

Lewes Road

I MILE ON LEFT
HAYBERGH FARM

Gospels Farm

DITCHLING BEACON

Ditchling Common Lane

High Street

South Street

Beacon Road

Court Gardens Farm

E

N ← → S

W

Weat Street

KEYMER & HASSOCKS

Ditchling

Above: Father

Right: Mother

Insurance Agent and a Master Butcher. My father and his brother Dennis, who lived in Folders Lane, did contracting together. One of their biggest jobs was carrying loads of chalk and flints from the Downs to a site at Street where the Gallops was built.

Old Land Pond, Keymer, which stood very near the Old Land Mill

Old Land Mill,
Ditchling

Doris, Gordon, Vena, Iris and John at
Gospels Farm 1921

13

A picture of feeding time at Gospels Farm entered for the WD Competition
by A Haywrd of Wick Farm Cottage, Ditchling

My sister, Doris, with borther Gordon
and sister Vena in the pram at Gospels
Farm in the early 1920s

Anne of Cleves House, Ditchling,
which was once lived in by several
families is now one residence

My father's first marriage did not last long owing to the sad death of his first wife. He then met and married my mother. She worked at a large house on the common called Fragbarrow which I believe, for a while, was owned by Mr Maynard, a Burgess Hill Solicitor. Unfortunately in 1918 Bulls Barn Farm was put up for sale.

My parents then moved the family to Gospels Farm Ditchling. At one time it was owned by monks from Lewes. When the monks collected their rates and tithes in the area they would stay at Gospels. It is noticeable that all the fields on the farm were named after Apostles. I was born there in December 1919 and my brother Dennis eighteen months later.

Gospels was a lovely parcel of land and for several years we had a very happy time. My father started a milk business from scratch, which soon grew into a profitable gallonage. Gospels Farm cottage had apparently suffered from subsidence and large pillars were added for support. There were two downstairs rooms plus a dairy. A spare room of wooden structure was added which was used for storage or as a bedroom or playroom. We had a large, comfortable kitchen that was heated by an iron grate which kept us warm. My mother used to always be cooking and washing. The front room faced south with a clear view of the South Downs. It looked out onto the orchard. We had a lovely selection of eating apples with plenty of cookers and keepers. This room was heated by a small open fire. There were family photographs on the wall and two lovely pictures titled 'Morning in the Highlands' and 'Evening in the Highlands'. A stairway led up to the two bedrooms. The smaller one, which faced south, was occupied by my parents. The larger room was shared by us children. It's window faced the nearby road so we were well aware of goings on. Part of the Cowstall joined the rear of the cottage and sometimes at night we heard them, the clanking of chains or one of them bellowing.

The dairy was spotless. The milk was strained through a muslin cloth. The bottles of various sizes, were washed by hand in hot soda water and then rinsed in cold water and then drained on a stone surface. Deliveries were twice daily in sealed bottles, measures of one quart, one and a half pints, one pint and half pint. Butter, eggs and cream were also supplied and special milk for infants and invalids. Thin and clotted cream was skimmed of the large pans. The floor was red brick which was kept well scrubbed. The waste water from the kitchen and dairy ran underground directly to a ditch by the roadside. Our toilet facilities were just the country norm at the time, a short distance in the garden stood a little shed.

Mother worked hard helping wherever possible, plus caring for the needs of four young children. A number of good Jersey and Guernsey cows were kept, plenty of chicken and ducks and of course, cats! Several of our customers had their milk measured straight from the can to their jug. I know my father was generous, filling the measure and an extra drop. In the early days my brother Gordon used to deliver milk before school and at weekends, while my sister Doris was learning weaving at Mrs Mairet's, next door. As we got older we all had our jobs to do.

My mother was popular in the village, belonging to the Women's Institute, attending fetes and other charitable occasions. When my sister Iris was three and a half she caught Meningitis. She was very ill but later made a full recovery. Unfortunately soon afterwards a Scarlet Fever epidemic broke out resulting in everyone catching the fever.

During the summer months my mother and helpers served teas on the lawn. Farmhouse cream teas proved popular, meaning extra work but providing extra money. Often the people taking tea would like to see the animals and have a walk around the farm, sometimes feeding the chicken and ducks as well as buying farm produce.

My father took the milkround in a tricycle, which was quite a lot to push uphill. One day he told me this story. Early one morning he was awakened by Mr Carey calling outside his bedroom window. Mr Carey explained to my father that the great painter, Sir Frank Brangwyn, was very ill and he required ,some milk straight from the cow. As it was a special request my father duly obliged and apparently Sir Frank survived.

Mr Carey, whom I mentioned, lost most of his money in the Farrow's Bank smash. He made a fresh start doing odd jobs.They lived at Sand Pit Gardens where he grew vegetables and flowers. He then started a small greengrocers, the last in line of the houses in the high street, next to the Bull Hotel. The Carey's were always very kind to us and my father sold them lots of vegetables.

At Christmas, if we were very lucky, some of the customers gave us boxes of sweets or chocolates and other presents. As a family we had a collecting box in which we saved money for a charity called the Young Helpers League. Every Christmas a large party was held for all the helpers at the Downs Hotel in Keymer. It was something that we all looked forward to and enjoyed.

It was wonderful at Gospels, lots of people visited and we were safe to roam wherever we pleased. The nearest house to us then was 'The Weavers' owned by Mrs Mariet. Also near us was 'Old Paygate Cottage' which was let for six pence a week and the house opposite us was called 'Gunsfield'. Early one morning I heard the 'clippity clop' of heavy horses approaching and someone singing 'The Farmer's Boy' at the top of his voice. My mother informed me that it was Mr Tanswell. He was well known in the village and he worked as a carter for Mr Saunders who ran Ditchling Court and Park Barn Farm. Several years later I saw Mr Tanswell playing the melodeon and singing in a local pub.

Lewes Road, Ditching. Now all houses and a new school

Sandrock Inn, Ditchling

Haymaking

17

A lovely old photograph of Mayston's Stores, West Street, Ditchling

Dymocks Manor, East End Lane, Ditchling

18

The field at Gospels Farm where Ditchling Cricket club played for seven years from 1922-23. Note the cricket screens

At haymaking time ladies from the village used to roll over the swathes with long handled wooden rakes. Some used to help put the hay in cocks (large heaps) ready for carting. We loved travelling out into the field in the empty wagons. The ladies would wear bonnets to protect them from the sun. We had a nice old mare at the time called Violet.

My father employed Mr Linsor, a traveller, on a temporary basis to do odd jobs for him. For a short while he slept in the feed shed. He seemed a very pleasant man but my father wanted him to move on. They were always arguing about it, so Mr Linsor moved to an unused pigsty on the farm. It was well built with new railway sleepers and a corrugated tin roof. There was a concrete entrance. Mr Linsor seemed to be settled. He had a large pile of old sacks and a couple of coats for a bed.

Fred Edwards was the local Post Master and played local cricket

VILLAGE SEARCH.

70 People Hunt For Missing Woman.

DITCHLING TRAGEDY.

The mysterious disappearance of a well known Ditchling woman, Mrs. Sarah Alice Stenning, aged 47, of the Gospels Farm, the wife of Mr. Lewis Stenning, a dairyman, was cleared up yesterday morning, when the tragic discovery of her body lying in a ditch, was made by a party of searchers.

Mrs. Stenning, the mother of four children, was a prominent member of the Ditchling Women's Institute. It is understood that she had been in ill-health for some time. She retired as usual on Tuesday night, but on wakening the following morning, her husband discovered she was missing. No note was left to explain her absence, and it was thought that she was too physically weak to walk far, and she carried no money.

When the police were informed, P.S. W. Hambleton, a constable, Mr. Ashby, and two other civilians made a search, throughout Wednesday, of the whole of the immediate countryside. The Downs were scoured, and it seemed that every possible place of concealment, even the bushes which abound round Ditchling Beacon, were thoroughly searched, without success. Mr. Ashby continued the search still further and could find no trace of the missing woman.

Great Search Party.

By Saturday, every one in the village was becoming very concerned for Mrs. Stenning, who was a very popular person. No clues could be found, and Mr. C. Cutress and Mr. C. Cottingham, two local tradesmen, decided to organize a great search party. Practically all the male inhabitants of the picturesque old world village were about early yesterday morning, and, gathering at Mr. Cutress' tea room about nine o'clock, and were speedily mobilised into small search parties. In all, 70 men took part. At 9.15 the first party, under the direction of Mr. R. Sellens, left West-street, the principal thoroughfare of the village, to make a complete search of the countryside between the Drove and Lodge Hill. A little later, a further party, in the charge of Mr. G. Davey, left for the direction of Keymer, while others, under Mr. Cutress and Mr. F. Wood, began searches towards The Nye and the foot of the Downs. Everybody displayed great vigilance, and no nook or cranny, bush or hedge, was left before a thorough exploration had been carried out. No effort was spared to find Mrs. Stenning, if she was anywhere in the district.

Lying Face Downwards.

Just before ten o'clock, a party of searchers, many of whom were ex-Service men, made the discovery. A young lad, named Hemsley, who had joined Mr. Wood's party, was walking along by the ditch on the edge of the old, disused coach-road which adjoins Nye Shaw coppice, when he saw an object lying in the ditch. Mr. Mitchell was the next on the scene and further investigation showed that it was the body of Mrs. Stenning, lying face downwards at the bottom of the ditch. She had been dead for some time. Mrs. Stenning was attired only in her ordinary working apparel, and wore no hat or coat.

P.S. Hambleton afterwards removed the body to the Bull Hotel, Ditchling. The actual spot where the body of the unfortunate woman was found was about a quarter of a mile from her home. In view of the fact that no one seems to have seen Mrs. Stenning immediately before she seemingly collapsed, it would appear that she left her home during the night.

After the discovery had been made, the search parties gradually came in from their various "beats."

News of the discovery quickly spread, and general regret was felt in the village, as the story of the tragic end to the mystery was related. All kinds of fears had been entertained for Mrs. Stenning, as the days went by, though it was hoped, even until yesterday morning, that she would be found alive. There was nothing to indicate that she had left the village.

Blind Lane going sharp right to Rolls Croft, the entrance to Borrows Platt.
Cricketer Mr Borrower was mentioned in the book 'The Cradle of Cricket'

The old village pond where villagers skated during the bad winters
when it was covered with ice

East End Farm, East End Lane, Ditchling. This was once the farmhouse

East End Lane where Mr Lancelot Knowles lived. He played cricket for Kent and
Sussex. The two cottages shown are now one property

Us children used to visit him (not if my mother knew it and sometimes he would give us a few chips that he had been cooking. Eventually my father was really firm and after a heated argument my father threatened to call Mr Linsor finally packed his few belongings into a sack and stated going to Pouchlands Workhouse. Later, by strange coincidence, I nursed there when it became a hospital. Referring to Mr Linsor however and there were lots like it, fancy, carrying all their worldly possessions in a small sack and living in barns etc..

In his younger days we had Val Kilbride living in a caravan on the farm. He learnt his weaving skills at Mrs Mairet's, our next door neighbour. I was very young and was wandering up towards the fields when Val Kilbride passed me. He was the first person I saw to jump a five barred gate. The photograph was kindly lent to me by his daughter Jenny.

Another character I remember who visited Gospels twice a week was Mr Simmonds. He was a bright, cheerful man. He used to work for Holmans in Burgess Hill. Mr Simmonds came with his horse and covered wagon. He brought our bread and flour, maize and meal for the fowl, linseed cake for the odd fattening animals and slabs of cow cake. We used to break up the cow cake in a machine for the milking cows.

My mother was suffering from an illness, she did not go out so much and was always nervy, breathless and tired. For a few weeks she had to go away and stay for hospital treatment. My sisters Vena and Iris and my brother Dennis and I went to stay at six, High Street, Ditchling with an elderly lady called Mrs Muddle. It was pretty basic in those days. If we wanted to go to the toilet, we had to go through next door's kitchen to a loo at the top of the garden. Later we actually moved next door. Sometimes we used to stay with Mrs Cornell, a friend of my mother, at Hassocks. There was a nice garden and nearby fields where we could roam or play, all of these are now houses. The local blacksmith, Jolly Jack Sayers as we called him, made us iron hoops with a hook to steer them with. Mr Seal, the local carpenter, made hobby horses for us to play on.

The Ditchling football and cricket clubs used to play in the fields at Gospels. There was never a dull moment. Although the cricket wicket was chained off, often the cattle would enter before the game and the cricketers would spend time clearing the cow pats off the pitch. I have seen 'green whites' when some had been missed. Football was played at Gospels for several years.

One day big Jack Bannister went into bat and a new cricket ball was being used. The first ball bowled to him was well pitched up and Jack hit it straight into the pond. Bill Kenning used to play cricket at Gospels too but I will be saying more about him later. The football team promised to always take their nets down just in case an animal got caught up in them. On one occasion they forgot and I found a sheep struggling in the net. I ran and fetched my father. He was furious and cut the net to pieces with his pocket knife to free the frightened animal. After that they were always taken down.

One very bad winter I set off with my brothers and sisters to deliver the milk. Snow was caked onto the road so we used a sledge. We were delivering to the road approaching the Beacon and Underhill Lane. We managed to get up to Coombedown House, but from there the road was impassable owing to a six foot snow drift. We had to climb into the field and go round it in order to deliver to Mr Williams's house, further down the road called 'Saillards'. There was to be a bad fire at Coombedown

Road men in Underhill Lane

Above: Old bottle top
Right: The author with some old milk churns from Gospels Farm

24

Ditchling cross roads in quieter days

Rolls Croft, Ditchling.
The harness makers shop where my father worked in the early days

The butchers shop on the left, Gatlands the first house on the right and next to this,
Sir Frank Brangwyns property.

North End, Ditchling

High Street, Ditchling. We lived at number 7, Chichester house is on the left

Mr Eade, landlord of the North Star taken
in Star Field

Mrs Eade and daughters who lived
at the North Star Inn

This is how I remember South Road, Ditchling. You can see the fieds where the larger houses were built

The Bull Hotel, Ditchling

Ditchling Common in quieter days

Above:
Ditchling crossroads. The butchers shop on the left was once the workhouse. Hoadleys sold not only groceries but cloth, nails and papers

Left:
The old smithy in East End Lane

East End Lane, Ditchling

L Jarratt driving the last flock of sheep through Ditchling

Top left:
St Margaret's Church,
Ditchling

Centre left:
'Preparing for home'

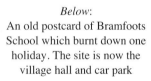

Below:
An old postcard of Bramfoots
School which burnt down one
holiday. The site is now the
village hall and car park

HOADLEYS Ltd., Burgess Hill, Tel. 2201

Funeral Directors and Monumental Masons,
FUNERALS CONDUCTED UNDER PERSONAL
SUPERVISION TO ALL PARTS.
ORDERS FOR MOURNING RECEIVE PROMPT AND CAREFUL ATTENTION.
(See Advt. on page 288).

House later on and lots of it had to be rebuilt. A large marl pit was found there in the early days.

By this time I had already started school. Like all beginners I felt a little uneasy but Miss Rose Brooker, the infants teacher, dispelled all that. It was all too much for one new arrival, he started to wet and he was stood in a sandtray until he could be moved to better facilities. I used to walk both ways to and from school, but if I could get to Keymer Girls' school in time I would catch Mr Bates. He delivered the morning milk with his pony and float and would often give me a lift for the rest of the journey to school. I hated the open road from Keymer to the Ditchling War Memorial especially if I had to walk it alone at dusk. I used to try and run that bit of road.

My mother often came to meet me but her health was deteriorating fast. I remember the last time I was to see her, she came and said her usual good night to us. Early the next morning my father was running about with a hurricane lamp saying that mother was missing. The neighbours and police were alerted and they searched all the locality. They found no trace of her at all. It was cold November and my mother apparently had gone out with no warm clothing. Different local people went out by day to search for her. By the weekend everyone was worried and a larger search was organised. Several parties set out.

Above:
South Street, with the old workhouse on the left and the downs in the background

Left:
My father's onions grown at Gospels

Below:
Common Lane (North Street) with the blacksmiths shop on the left where Jolly Jack made our iron hoops

Part of Ditchling Common near the Guild

I was at Sunday school when the news came. I was taught by Sarah Turner at the Ditchling Churchroom. George Edwards was teaching the elder group by the door. Someone came in and spoke to George and then he shook his head and went out. I knew then it was something to do with my mother. Sadly it was true, my mother had been found in a ditch, about a mile from our house, at the top of Nye Lane. At my mother's inquest Dr Eggar said she had had a valvular heart complaint for some time. Eventually she had become so worried that she was unable to cope. We had lost someone so good and loving to us and it was to make such a change to our lives.

Our Aunt came to look after us, she was strict but kind. She did not like the Gospels house. My brother Dennis and I went to school at Ditchling for a few months. Aunt got her way in the end and we moved to Hassocks, to quite a

Val Kilbride was the first person I saw to jump a five-bar gate. He learnt weaving at Mr Mairets next to Gospels and later formed the Guild at Ditchling Common with other craftsmen.

large house called Park View. It was situated opposite the Orchard Pleasure Gardens. I naturally returned to Hassocks school. I remember my teacher, Miss Clark, saying, "Dear John, you appear to have gone backwards!"..I am certain that it was due to the events that had taken place. It did not want thinking about.

Whilst at Hassocks we attended Keymer Sunday School and also Keymer Church. Mr Stevens was the Headmaster of Hassocks' school. I did not know him very well as I was in the infants at the time. I understand he was there for a great number of years. Mr Self took over and what a good man he proved to be. He enjoyed sport, had a lovely wife and their first child was born at the school house. Mr Self was very friendly with Mr Seal, a Hassocks' baker. He also took an interest in school sports. He played cricket for the Sussex County Team on one occasion, but did not have good fortune. Mr Self purchased two new cricket bats and other sports equipment for both the girls and the boys. The girls had very good netball and stool-ball teams. Mr Self did not stay in Hassocks long and moved on to Ringmer. A game of football was arranged between Hassocks and Ringmer Ringmer were the winners by 1-0. Mr Self's replacement at the school was Mr Hitchen. He soon took over the sports side for the boys.

Miss Parsons was an excellent teacher of long standing at Hassocks school.The pupils whom she taught liked and respected her.

Mr Hitchen joined the teaching staff. He had already taken over the sports side at Hassocks after Mr Self's departure. Our new head was Miss Emma Brooker, the sister of Miss Rose Brooker, the infants teacher. She was a strict disciplinarian and it was not long before I was to be disciplined by her.

By that time I had been captain of the cricket and football teams. Also I had a leaders house badge. There were houses called Allanby, Haig and Jellicoe. Whatever house you were in, a number of marks could be gained by good actions or lost by bad. Miss Brooker gave a strong warning, no one was to climb up onto the roof of the school shelter to retrieve tennis balls which became lodged there. The shelter was in the front playground. Her reason for this was that the wire surround was getting damaged when the balls were retrieved. On this particular playtime our ball got lodged on the roof. I had always been the one to be lifted up to get it. I was hesitant remembering what Miss Brooker had said. However the other boys encouraged me. "Come on John!" they shouted. "We will get you up there!" As no-one seemed to be about I agreed and to cheers, retrieved the ball. Before I climbed down I casually glanced around. There standing outside the front school door stood Miss Emma Brooker. She then turned and entered the school and we resumed our game.

Nothing had happened and I thought perhaps the new Head Mistress did not mean what she had said. Soon the whistle sounded the end of playtime and quickly and quietly we filed into the classroom. We were preparing for lessons to commence and then the 'Bomb' struck.

Miss Brooker looking red faced and angry called out, "John Stenning come to the front of the class!" I was a little alarmed as I proceeded to obey her orders. On arrival she said, "What were my instructions about climbing up onto the porch roof?" She came closer and before I could attempt to reply, I felt a bang around my left ear. It was not too bad. I then made the dreadful mistake of turning and grinning at the pupils in my class. Bang!1 I stumbled as my right ear received really stinging punishment. Her face reddened and her eyes looked wild. "Now grin!" she said, as her hand was raised for further punishment. I did not grin and realised I had more than met my match. I remained silent, she ordered me back to my seat and stated that I was to stay behind after the lesson. The class went very quiet and I rather hoped that the lesson would not end, fearing what was in store for me. However it did and when the class was dismissed I remained seated. "John! We will go into the side room." Miss Brooker said in a quieter tone. I obeyed and joined her. "I knew your father Lewis," she said, "we went to school together. I did not want to take the action I did, but now this incident is closed and forgotten, providing you behave. When I give instructions make sure they are carried out. You may keep your badges but your house team will lose five points." It was then that I made up my mind to try my best and from my future results I think this was borne out.

Mr Hitchen done lots for us, putting in his own time with sports. He also took a class in physical exercises. He started a debating class, also he was willing to give extra help and advice to pupils that needed it.

I enjoyed singing in Keymer church choir. We took part in the Lewes musical festival at the Corn Exchange and won third prize for singing a song called 'The Days Of The Week'. The seven of us each sang solo about a day of the week. The hall was crowded. I think our two best singers were Arthur Baskwell and Ernie Waldron, although we all tried hard. Arthur emigrated to New Zealand after the war. Ernie was to die soon after the war, which came as a great shock to me. He was a very good friend.

Ernie's parents were very kind to Dennis and myself during our school days. One day when we were round there listening to the cup final on ear phones for the very first time, Mr Waldron came in and called us. He pointed to an airship which was floating over the Adastra trees. It crashed soon after, the next day, I think. It was the R101, a German airship.

The Waldron's lived in a cosy, white cottage in the grounds belonging to Mr Stafford, who's house was nearer the road. Mr Waldron kept bees and often gave us a comb of honey to take home. He was a gardener for the Stafford family and took care of a lovely, large walled garden. In the garden shed in which his tools hung spotlessly clean, he had a boiler which used to send heated water around the walls of the garden, keeping out the frosts and providing some nice early vegetables for the house.

There was also a large apple orchard. He was a very generous man and when we were playing in the Adastra grounds he would bring out a large bag of apples and say "There you are lads, share them out amongst your-selves."

Eventually the Staffords' gave their big house to the community as a home for the elderly named the 'Eventide Home'. A few of us were invited to go there at Christmas to sing carols to the elderly folk. I was lucky enough to go twice. We had a lovely evening tea and a cake. The residents insisted on having a collection for us and before saying our goodbyes we sang them another carol, much to their appreciation.

The generous gifts given by the Staffords' to Hassocks must never be forgotten. For years Hassocks had tried to find facilities for recreation and all steps to secure ground had failed. Then Mr Stafford donated the Adastra recreation ground, accompanied by the Adastra hut. It had a beautiful gar-den of remembrance in which an oak sapling was planted by the council in 1926 to commemorate this wonderful gift. In 1928 the Staffords handed over their handsome house, Villa Adastra, together with over three acres of lovely gardens, to the Salvation Army. This was to be used as a home for forty poor, old people. They also gave one thousand pounds towards a new wing at the home in 1937. It was officially opened by Mrs Stafford.

Mr Jeffery was also a regular visitor to the school. He used to come on a motor cycle and was the school attendance officer. He went through the school register and used to call on parents to help iron out any disputes that might have arisen through the school or their children.

Soon after moving to Hassocks my father sold his milk business to Mr John Holman from North End, Ditchling. He then worked for him as his principal milk roundsman. The trouble with the milk business was that my father was unable to produce sufficient milk for his requirements. He fre-quently had to buy in to make up the amount needed. The milk that he pur-chased had to be paid for monthly but at that time there were several people in Ditchling requiring too much credit. If a monthly account was agreed and a book or bill presented it was often difficult to get the money paid for two or three months. Meaning there was not too much capital owing. He still managed to retain his small holding at Gospels Farm.

I was quite young when I worked for Mr Sinden at his chemist shop situ-ated at the Hurstpierpoint side of Hassocks. I used to deliver toiletries, med-icines, accumulators and other goods, evenings and weekends. Once when I was delivering at South Bank, an unmade road, on my poorly lit cycle, I did not notice that a hole had been dug and not filled in properly. My front

Form E.E. 314

EAST SUSSEX EDUCATION COMMITTEE.

For............

..................School. ....mixed...........Department.

Report for the Term ending July.........192.., on the work and conduct of

Age. 13 years 3 mths.   Average age of Class. 13 yrs. 11 mons.

SUBJECT.	Class Work	Term Examination		REMARKS
		Marks Possible	Marks Obtained	
Reading.		15	13.	
Recitation.	17	15	13	
Writing.	13	10	8	
Dictation.		20	16	Improving
Composition.	14	20	15	Spelling is the weakest subject
Literature.		20	19	
Eng. Language		50	40	
Geography.	18	50	34	
History.	19	40	20	
Arithmetic.	17		11	Has improved considerably
Drawing.		20	16	
Handwork.	48	50	1.4	
Needlework.		50		
Physical Exercises.	16	20	16	
	21.2	500	376	

Number of Pupils in class.... 19   Position in Class.... 2

Attendance: No of times School opened.......   No. of Absences.......

Conduct:

Work and progress :— ....

..................Head Teacher.

EAST SUSSEX EDUCATION COMMITTEE.

For..........

..................Council.........School. ....Mixed.........Department.

Report for the Term ending August 3rd.......1923....on the work and conduct of

Age. 13 yrs. 8 months.   Average age of Class. 13 yrs. 8 months.

SUBJECT.	Class Work	Term Examination		REMARKS.
		Marks Possible	Marks Obtained	
Reading.		10	8	
Recitation.				
Writing.		20	14	
Dictation.		50	36	
Composition.		40	39	
Literature.		50	33	
Eng. Language				
Geography.				
History.		40	40	
Arithmetic.		100	30	
			10	
Drawing.		20	16	
Handwork.				
Needlework.				
Physical Exercises.				

Number of Pupils in class.... 10   Position in Class. 1

Attendance: No of times School opened.... 33   No. of Absences.......

Conduct:

Work and progress :— ....

..................Head Teacher.

Hassocks Council School

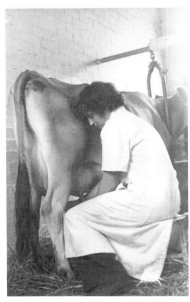

John Stenning aged 8 years

Sister Sheila hand milking at Gospels Farm after WWII

Sports for girls at Hassocks Cuncil School

Football at Hassocks School 1933-34

Sir Alan Cobham's Air Circus at Hassocks in the 1930s

Hassocks Council Infants School 1925-26

41

Park View, Hassocks where we lived opposite Orchard Gardens

Left:
Sharmans coal merchants
next to Keymer Church

Below:
Keymer village

wheel dropped into it, throwing medicines and accumulators across the road. The medicines were made up in quite large bottles so there was lots of damage, which took some sorting out. Mr Sinden was not too pleased.

I also went to the Band of Hope where a few well meaning people gave lectures and film slides on the dangers of alcohol. The evening ended with tea and cakes. The meeting was held at the old chapel next to Hassocks' school. We were asked to sign a pledge, which I did, but later it was broken.

Another of my school friends was Roy Langridge, the son of the local policeman. Every home cricket match at Clayton, we would walk through the cinder path, a track that follows the railway line to Clayton. On this particular Saturday we had arrived at the ground in good time and we were standing on the grass verge opposite the entrance to the cricket field, watching the traffic and the team arrive. Suddenly there was a loud bang. On looking towards the fork road at the bottom of Clayton Hill, I saw a car out of control hurtling towards us. It was an open touring car. Afterwards I learnt the driver had been thrown out and sustained injuries. Roy ran further up the grass verge, but I became rooted to the spot. I shall never know why but I must have momentarily lost consciousness. I woke up under the car with hot oil dripping on my trousers. I could hear lots of movement and shouting and then Roy said "Where's John?"

"I'm under here." I called.

A man's voice said, "Are you hurt?"

I remember replying, "I don't think so but oil is dripping on my trousers."

A face appeared under the car and said "We are going to pull you out by your feet, shout if it hurts."

Soon I was standing on my feet but shaking badly and saying "I'm alright." I was taken to Doctor Eggar's surgery in Hassocks. The Doctor had left to play cricket at the Adastra, apparently he was often called away and he came to examine me. I was still trembling from shock but nothing else appeared wrong with me.

"What are you going to do now?" the Doctor said.

"I would like to go back to my cricket" I replied.

"I'm taking you home." he said, giving me some tablets to take. He dropped me off at Parkview and explained to my stepmother that I was to rest and to call and see him in his surgery on Monday morning, but all was well.

The driver in the accident worked for Lady Demetre Hardy from Street, who was to open a fete at Patcham. She had forgotten something so he was sent back to collect it. The court found he was driving much too fast and he had been the cause of the accident.

Doctor Eggar has pulled teeth out for me before going to school. I once

43

had a bad milk fester. My finger was painful and throbbing. Mrs Eggar was talking to me but I noticed the doctor take something out of the drawer. "Give me your hand." the Doctor said, "and keep talking to Mrs Eggar." I then felt a slight graze and then relief. My finger had been lanced and after a dressing had been applied. I then went off to school.

Unfortunately I was to be expelled from the Keymer church choir. My brother Dennis and I were standing on the pavement opposite, which was Grinstead's grocery store. Lying in the gutter was a rotten potato. We were waiting for the Sunday school to open. I heard footsteps coming down the church steps and I rightly guessed it was the choir mistress. She was coming to open the Sunday school which was hidden by tall shrubs. As the footsteps approached I lobbed the juicy potato over the shrubs. I soon heard some squeals and the voice of the choir mistress say, "Come here whoever threw that." The next moment she appeared round the corner holding on to her hat with the remnants of the potato dripping off the wide brim onto her blue dress. I immediately apologised and using a clean handkerchief, I helped to remove the offending potato. "You are expelled from the choir and Sunday school," said the unhappy lady, "And I'll be calling to see your father." Naturally I went home and told him the news. Then a letter arrived saying I had meaningly said sorry to her but she requested I made a public apology at Sunday school. This I did not want to do. My Sunday school teacher, Miss Eastwood tried to persuade me but I said no. I lost my choir pay which amounted to a few shillings and that was that.

It was not long after this unhappy escapade at Sunday school that Miss Brooker read out a letter from the 'Evening Star', a paper then quite widely circulated. It stated that John Stenning had won a Jack Hobbs' bat for the best school bowling average. They gave one bat away each week, one for bowling and one for batting. I was pleased and the head teacher went on to say a school outing would be arranged to go to London and I could go to Jack Hobbs' sports shop in Fleet Street to pick the bat of my choice together with a certificate. My brother came, George Holman, Arthur Baskwell, Rex King and Ernie~ Waldron. It was a mixed outing and we saw many of the London sights. Whilst the party was visiting the Tower, Mr Hitchen and I went to Fleet Street. There we met the great cricketer himself, who wished me good luck.

Jack Hobbs was such a nice, quiet gentleman. I saw him later watching a match at Sussex County cricket ground. After he finished playing he retired to Hove and was a frequent visitor, even though his sight was failing. Rex King who played in our school team later sent in a better bowling performance than mine, but unluckily, he did not get a bat. We met a few years later, just after the war, at a match at Westmeston and Streat. Rex was playing for Sayers Common CC. He clouted my first ball I bowled to him, for six and grinning he said "That's some of my own back."

A very clever pupil at Hassocks school was Dorothy Stacy, later to become Mrs Moore. Dorothy won a scholarship to a secondary school at Lewes, I think she was first to achieve this.

Being so near the pleasure gardens, we enjoyed 'All the Fun of the Fair' without going there. It was amazing to see the streams and streams of people who would wait for admittance on a sunny or busy day. I did go up and help Robin Doubleday sometimes with the boats on the lake. It got me a few shillings pocket money and it was quite a nice job. We also used to wait for Robin to bring out his set of stumps, with a bat and ball, so we could enjoy a game of cricket in the Adastra Park. He was the very popular son of the owner. Sadly he was a victim of World War Two at Arnhem, dying much too young. Living next door to us (No.4 Parkmore Terrace) was a lady named Miss Mary Towner, who was both deaf and dumb. One morning however she received a "fright" recovering she felt a hoarseness in her throat and suddenly Mary could speak and her hearing had returned. By this time I had two more younger sisters, Jean and Sheila.

If you were lucky enough to get picked, a good job was as a Ball Boy at the Weald Tennis club during the Summer holidays. This was a very high class tournament in those days. Some very talented players took par~ One had to keep alert because of constant supervision. The club was founded in 1920. It was stated an excellent site had been secured near the Hassocks Station, five grass courts and two hard courts, also a club house or pavilion, were provided. The costings were being met by generous donations, subscriptions and other means.

As some of the apples were nicely ripe in Mr Turner's Newlands Farm, Okley Lane in Keymer, two of my friends and myself decided to go scrumping. Everything was quiet and we entered the orchard by a gate. I was up a tree collecting a few when my friend mentioned that there were some nice juicy ones to be found under a tree several yards away. Suddenly I heard someone shouting and I saw the foreman running towards my pals who hastily made a dash across the fields towards the Adastra. I watched them running and then the foreman gave up the chase. I had plenty of time to get down from the tree with the apples. I went out of the entrance to the road, turned into 'Lover's Walk' and joined my friends on the Adastra. We sat down and had a good laugh and a good 'munch'. Another place we used to visit every year was the Burnt house in Underhill Lane, Ditchling where everything was growing wild. There were apples, plums, bullice, blackberries and wild strawberries.

Whilst at Hassocks I was a member of Mr Beecher Shand's Church Lads Brigade. That brings back some happy memories. Mr Shand lived in a large house near the station approach which was called 'Holmwood' with large

Stone and Pound Crossways, Hassocks

Clayton Park Hotel, West Side Hassocks Station, now closed for several years

Above: St Cosmos and St Damien Church, Keymer

Below: Hassocks Congregational Church where I signed the pledge

grounds that have all been built on. The Church Lads Brigade hut was built in the grounds and was well equipped with ropes, wall bars, parallel bars, a horse, mats and everything for physical training. When we gave a display, help came from the late Reg Cragg and Mr Hammond. They were both very good instructors.

Part of the Keymer and Clayton Royal British Legion stands on part of the site of the Brigade hut. When I was about thirteen years of age, I was left a Boys Brigade Belt by William (Bill) Arnold who died at Roberts Bridge with T.B. I treasured it for a long time.

For a couple of summer holidays I worked for Miss Haig who was Earl Haig's sister. She lived at the Dale House. There was a bell on the outside which had to be rung for deliveries or admittance. When the late Jack Hughes, who used to tend to her various animals went on holiday, I liked doing it. Miss Haig was a strange but kind lady. She kept geese, chicken, ducks and guinea fowl. Mr Lamey was the gardener living in a small bunga-low nearby. I once remember he gave me a ride in his motor bike and side car. It was the first time I had been in a side car.

Just a little further up the road to Miss Haig lived two strange old ladies, the Miss Thunders. Their large house called Woodlands looked very bleak and although I had to deliver there a few times, I never got an answer and left the articles in the outside porch. I understand for a time they taught at Sunday School but I was never taught by them.

By this time we had moved back to Ditchling and after looking round the village, I remember at the time there were three houses to let, two to be let or sold. We finished up at 7 High Street which was a comfortable house. The rent was 6 shillings and 9 pence. There was a cellar and scullery, to which the residents of number 6 had right of way to the garden and toilet. It had quite a large kitchen and front room, four bedrooms and an out house which was once a tiny dwelling for storage. In the kitchen there was a large iron grate. My stepmother made all kinds of home made wine which was very potent. It was stored in the cellar. Our toilet was also up the garden.

When I was about twelve years old, Miss Lindfield asked my father if I could go and sleep at her house. On the corner of Ditchling Crossroads. She had recently lost her mother and she hated being alone in such a large build-ing at night. I was reluctant but agreed. At about this time my sister, Vena, was completing her nursing training S.R.N at St. Bartholomew's Hospital in London, although she only had a council school education, leaving at four-teen years of age. She also won the students prize. Later she nursed in Nairobi and had a house built there naming it "Ditchling".

Lindfield's had been a butchers shop for a very long time. It was then rented by Mr Jeffery the Ditchling butcher and later I worked there. Guy Thornton, a very popular man, was the manager. Miss Lindfield told me her father was born in Ditchling in 1848 and had carried on the butcher's business there for many years. He died in 1928 and had celebrated his golden wedding there in 1921. The premises were on the site of the former Ditchling workhouse.

Miss Lindfield also told me that her mother was the daughter of Mr Greenyer who was a pastor for 28 years at the Beaulah Baptist Chapel in Ditchling. She showed me an old photograph of a cord across the road (east to west) and hanging from it were marrow bones, a meat cleaver and other butchers tools including blue apron when her parents returned to

Ernie Waldron, John Stenning and Arthur King after 1927 in the Adastra

the shop after their honeymoon in 1871, Miss Lindfield was, I understand, the only child. Her father was the first Ditchling tradesman to have gas installed. Their meat and sausages were sold over a large area. "You ought to have seen the large joints of meat my father cut for the many dinners held at the Bull Hotel and also for the Pouchlands workhouse (later Pouchlands Hospital)," she told me. The workhouse had the lesser parts of the meat - rolled brisket very cheap, perhaps 3d or 4d per pound. It was an outlet for their breast of lamb which could be boned and rolled or stewed. Their own slaughtering was also carried out on the premises.

I hated sleeping there and would wake early and go down to Gospels and start milking the cows. Father was often surprised by the amount I had done on his arrival. I forgot to mention whilst at Hassocks my brother, Dennis or I would take our four wheeled home-made truck up to the coal wharf over the Hurstpierpoint side of Hassocks station and for 10p they would fill us up with coke, 1/- for coal. It was handy as we often ran short. How things have changed, I used to hate going to school wearing patches on my trousers, now it's part of fashion with jeans.

I was well settled in at school as my reports were to show. At twelve and a half I was third in class and at thirteen years and eight months in my last report, I came first in class. Although for a long time I had been anxious to leave school and get to work, when the time came to say goodbye to the teachers I did so with a heavy heart.

I left school on a Friday and on the Sunday I started work. Early jobs were easy to get but although I was only fourteen I was expected to work with the men. I had hardly any time off and precious little in the way of wages at the end of the week to show for it. I started at 10/-, so it was quite sensible, should a job for more money or more time off become available, off you went. Naturally the sport I had enjoyed was reduced to evenings or special days off.

My first job involved a small early morning milk round to Westmeston and it's approaches. One customer's order apart from the milk was half a pint of fresh cream. This had to be delivered daily by 7.30 AM. I remember it was a dreadfully, cold, frosty morning with black ice on the roads. Realising the bad conditions I hurried to work, setting out in good time to make this special delivery by the time required. As it was quite hilly country and very slippery, I had to walk long parts of the way. I arrived with two quarts of milk and half a pint of fresh cream, knowing I might be minutes late. Knocking at the door I was quickly told, "One quart only and as you're late you can take the cream back!" What a reward for trying.

Mr Vetz was the owner of Court Gardens Farm which he purchased somewhere around the First World War. Mr Muggeridge was a good friend of his and as manager, was given a free hand. The cow stall was made from an old army hut from WWIand provided handsome housing for 70 or 80 cows. Mr Mggeridge loved dealing, but unfortunately after many years he was left with some animals not quite up to scratch. However, the land was very good. I understand that many years ago, the monks were there, and the farmhouse is very old. It was run as a mixed farm, principally pasture. One lovely field, mostly kept under the plough was called 'The Hop Garden' and at the end of the old cart shed once stood a cart house.

I soon left that employment hearing that Mr Muggeridge of Court Gardens Farm, Ditchling, required a cowman, as he had someone away with a long illness. At that time he could not offer permanent employment, however I received five shillings more, but the hours were 5.00 AM to 5.00PM. I liked Mr Muggeridge and the job, but the young gentleman whose job I had taken over proved to recover his health much quicker than expected. He was a nice young chap, a parson's son learning the trade. Mr Muggeridge wanted me to stay in another capacity, but I decided to get another job where I could play cricket on Wednesdays and also football. I received 10/- extra in my last pay packet from Mr Muggeridge containing a little note saying, should a job arise to suit me at the farm he would only be too pleased to take me on. That was two jobs in a few months.

My next job was as a butcher boy at the butcher's on the Crossroads at Ditchling. I had slept over the top of the shop in my school days. Guy Thornton was the manager there. The money was not so much but I had Wednesdays and Sundays off. This enabled me to play cricket on Wednesdays for Ditchling and often on a Sunday for the Bill Kennings Lodge Hill Xl. It proved an interesting job. In those days I had to call for orders in the village and deliver them on the same day. I did the round which was quite extensive, on a bicycle, three times a week. It covered

Ditchling common, Spatham Lane, Ditchling Village, Westmeston and Clayton including the windmills. I quite enjoyed it. I served some very nice customers. There was always plenty of cleaning to do in the shop. I also quickly learnt to pick and dress game and poultry. I helped to mix and make both pork and beef sausages, beef being the cheaper of the two. Another job I liked was making pressed beef - I also liked eating some of it, should the chance arrive. Guy, the manager, was very good to me. Not only would he put me in touch with a few odd jobs in the evenings but he would some-times let me off early on a Saturday. When he paid me there was always a well hung piece of steak, chops, or a few sausages for extras. I was expected to look smart and clean and he showed me the correct presentation of meat. I always used a clean tray and cover for the meat when making a delivery.

Whilst working there I was asked by the Ditchling Cricket Club if I would like to attend the Sussex County Cricket Ground at Hove for one weeks coaching. Many clubs used this facility if twelve pounds could be raised for the County Club. Ditchling done it by Whist Drives which were very popular in those days and a member was chosen for coaching. I had saved and gathered most of my gear but none of the protection stuff was used then. Although I was so young it was a wonderful experience.

The Sussex coach at that time was George Cox senior. The professionals at the nets that week were Jack Nye, Alf Tuppen and Jim Hammond who also played football for Fulham. Also there was a great friend of mine, Tim Killick. He was on one months trial but he preferred to continue working for the press. Apart from being struck by a fast rising ball (where it hurts!) from Jack Nye, I seemed to get along alright. I was surprised the following year when I was asked to go again. Unfortunately an elderly Clayton family were proving to be difficult with regard to their meat deliveries, which meant I was often sent back to get their meat changed, "Too fat!", was the cry. On this particular Wednesday, I was due to play cricket in an away match departing at 1.30pm. In those days we travelled in Mr George Turner's lorry. The seats were made to enable them to be put in and removed quite easily. It was a bit of a shaky ride but I looked forward to it.

On arrival at this customer I hoped the piece of steak would be satisfacto-ry. I walked up the long garden path to the back door and knocked. After a short delay the door was opened by the daughter. I politely said, "Good morning!" but the good lady's first remark was not encouraging. "It's too fat!" she said. Then turning she called out up the passage, "Mother! The butcher is here but it's fat again."

"Bring it to me to look at." I heard the mother call and then she came shuffling out of a nearby room. She met the daughter and after messing about and deliberating the old lady said, "It's too fat butcher, take it back."

I was annoyed and hurried up the path to my bicycle and started to take

Burgess Hill Waterworks, Clayton, Sussex.

Above: Burgess Hill Waterworks, Clayton
Below: Farm and pond, Clayton

Farm & Pond, Clayton, Sussex.

the right fork of the road back to Ditchling. After cycling about 300 yards down the road, I stopped, propped the cycle up by the hedge and taking the offending meat (which meant cricket or no cricket) I sat down by a small pond. I took out my pen knife, in those days I always carried one and carefully I trimmed off most of the little bits of fat. I then turned it over the other side to which I gave a little bit of attention. It looked quite good, although there was little wrong in the first place. I sat down for a further fifteen minutes, before returning to the customer. I half ran and hurried up the garden path, panting as though I had been rushing about. I knocked and waited. The mother and daughter greeted me together. I managed to tell them, as I handed over the meat for their inspection, how I had been as quick as I could as I did not want their lunch to be delayed or spoilt. "What a lovely bit of steak, why can't Guy send us meat like this in the first place? Thank you butcher." I chuckled to myself as I hurried back up the path. On arrival the shop had been scrubbed up and I caught the cricket lorry driven by a cheerful smiling Alf Turner, his father, George, came as umpire.

We had another good laugh at Jefferies, the other butcher's shop in the village. It was at the top of the High Street, on the corner of East End Lane. Mr Jefferies had employed Jack for a long time. He was an excellent all round butcher, shopman, slaughterman and rounds man. He was a real jovial chap and enjoyed his half pint. He did deliveries at Keymer, Hassocks and Hurstpierpoint in a pony drawn butcher's cart. The pony's name was Brandy. Mr Jefferies thought at times, the round was taking too long. One day he said to Jack after a later than usual return, "One day I am coming with you to see what you get up to." The days went by and nothing happened and Jack hoped he had forgotten about it.

As Jack was loading his meat in the cart one day, out of the blue, Mr Jefferies stated that he was coming on the round and so they set off. Jack laughingly said that 'Brandy was putting her best foot forward' and they were both swaying to the movement of the vehicle, along the stretch of open road approaching Keymer, nearing the Greyhound public house. Jack tried to keep her on the straight course but Brandy turned in for her 'elevenses'. Jack adjusted the situation and turned out to get back on track to start deliveries. With no hindrances the round was completed in good time and they started on their homeward journey through Hassocks. As they approached the Greyhound Inn, Brandy tried to pull over again. "Now I know why the round takes so long!", barked the governor. However there was no sad ending as Jack continued to work and give continued good service to Mr Jefferies.

Everything went quite well but being young I was always on the look out and what happened next made me make up my mind a little more quickly. There was still a slaughter house which went with the shop. It was a horri-

The Church Lads Brigade on the left in the early 1920s

The Church Lads Brigade Hall where Keymer and Clayton BL stands

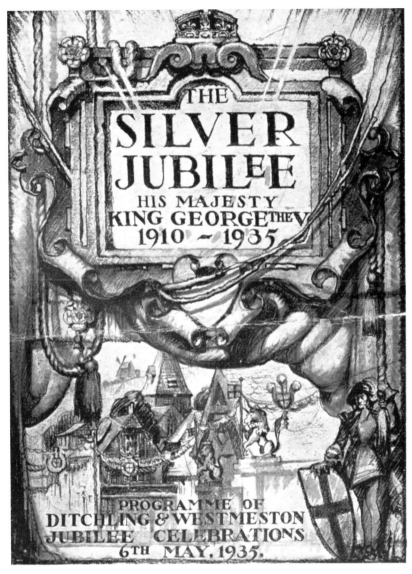

ble place. There were still the pens where the doomed animals made their last temporary stay. There was also a large pit where the odd parts of entrails went. This was covered by sawdust which had been swept from the shop floor and the droppings from the animals were also added. They were always kept down but it often got infested by rats. I often opened the doors and sent them scurrying away. Also the drawings of the poultry and game were placed there. It was emptied whenever it became necessary or when spare time was available. Mr Jefferies, like a lot of butchers in those days, would run their own bullocks and sheep. He had a little holding of several fields near, which is called Shirleys. In those days it was fashionable to have really fat bullocks and sheep. The day came for me to go slaughtering. It was a terrible experience, the dreadful squealing of the pigs and the blood. For a joke they tried to blood me and I hated every

Sister Vena
Queen Victoria District Midwife 1942

moment of it. "Never again!", I said and "That's that!" So after a short time with the butchers I was quite happy at first but this bad experience meant that I had made up my own mind to leave.

I was to spend a short while at East End Farm, working for my brother-in-law, Peter and my sister, Iris. It was one of the best jobs I had, there always seemed to be a super atmosphere. The work was hard and varied. A good dairy herd had been started, potatoes, corn and mangels were the crops. Peter and his father came from Caldy Island and started a very good dairy herd by buying some lovely, special foundation Guernsey cows from Court Gardens Farm. Peter used to say, expensive but worth it. Another Grand Short Horn was purchased from a well known Streat family, the Osborns. That is what they named her. Peter lost his father soon after coming to Ditchling and he was left in charge. He was a lovely, quiet person and certainly worked hard. He was very anxious to learn and we used to attend evening lectures at Plumpton Agricultural College. Some of the lectures were given by Mr Jessie, who was the principal- of the college. Tom soon came to join his brother and I really knew that three of us may be too many working at the farm.

One day a new cart horse arrived. It was only on trial from a horse dealer in Burgess Hill (Mr Woolgar). We called him 'Baldy' because he was always rubbing himself sore on the gates and fences. He had only been at the farm for a few weeks when Peter handed me the head stall, telling me to get the horse in. As I had been known to ride the others Peter gave me this warning, "Don't attempt to ride this one, he's young and not fully broken". So I set off. I also carried a few bits of cow cake which all animals seem to take to. Naturally I approached him quietly and I offered him the cake, which he took readily. I then rubbed his forehead and patted him. I soon had the head stall on him and he stood so still and appeared very friendly. Nearby was a heap of soil as we had dug out a ditch a few days previously. It was not long afterwards I made what may have been a terrible mistake. I lead Baldy up to the lump of soil and from there I had no trouble at all getting on his back. He stood quite still. Suddenly he reared up and I was flung right up in the air, landing in the ditch that we had recently dug out. Baldy galloped off in the direction of the farm. I had left the field gate open and he met Peter in the farm yard. I was shaken and dazed, muddy and wet. However I got to my feet and although feeling pain I climbed out of the ditch and started to make my way to the farm. I had not got far before I saw Peter coming through the open gate, the entrance to the field I was in. He hurried towards me and when I told him what had taken place, he 'threw the verbal book' at me. As I was in pain he took me up to the house where we sat down and had a cup of tea. Peter then said, "Did you think you were one of those jockeys you talked to me about!" Brother Tom who had joined us laughed, "That will larn you," he said.

Just before I was to leave the farm we entered for a 'clean milk' competition in a widely circulated paper called 'The Dairy Farmer'. The representatives called round at three different milking times to see the standard of our work and to take milk samples. The judges voted us the winners, much to our delight. Our photographs were in the paper and we received a cash prize

When the butcher and his wife returned from thier honeymoon, his apron and tools had been strung across the road. Told to me by Miss Lindfield and drawn by Andrew Stenning

Two views of Westmeston village which lies 1½ miles from Ditchling

Westmeston parish church

The parish church in Underhill Lane, Clayton

with which we had a small celebration supper.

On Sunday mornings I went down to Walnut Tree cottage in East End Lane where the Knowles family lived. They were nice, friendly people, keen foot beaglers and I used to clean the beagling shoes for the three of them, for which I was paid 2/6. Mr Knowles was the secretary of the Sussex County Cricket Club and he had played county cricket for both Sussex and Kent. He became president of Brighton Foot Beaglers and also Ditchling Cricket Club. He was a kind gentleman. Unfortunately the number of beagling shoes that needed cleaning used to increase in numbers. They were thick with mud and I often thought the extra pairs must have come from visiting beaglers. It was now late spring and the breeding season beagling had ended for the year. Mr Knowles saw me in the village and told me that they wanted to see me again at the County ground. I said as much as I would like to go I thought it would be fairer if another member went as I was sent last year. However I was picked to go by Ditchling Cricket Club. I tried to arrange an early payment from the farm but they were unable to give it to me as money was very short at that time. I went for coaching only on the Monday and Tuesday and then popped~round to find out about the money. It was not forthcoming so I went back to work. Mr Knowles was disappointed and several people said they would have helped me if they had known. It was left that if at any time I had three days off an arrangement could be made that I could continue the coaching.

As I expected Peter said three were too many on the farm and I should try to find something else suitable. If I had any spare time and they needed help they would always be glad for me to help them out. We continued to

Jack and Jill windmills at Clayton

A graveyard for farm wagons

go to the college lectures together, remaining the best of friends. They also offered to teach me to drive in the old Morris car they shared between them at the time. I was becoming unsettled at home and had made up my mind and leave. I had no bother getting a job as the local farmer, John Muggeridge asked me to go and see him. In his orchard he had an old railway carriage and I thought if I got the job with him he may let me live in it. However I was building castles a little too quickly. I was offered a good job, which paid 28/- per week plus overtime. When it was possible, occasionally I could play cricket or football. I asked if I could live in the caravan but he said abruptly, "No!" I took his confidence and told him that I wanted to leave home and look after myself. He promptly said, "Why don't you come and live in, there

The author with his brother-in-law, Peter Alford, at East End Farm 1935. his is now a wild life park lanscaped by Michael

Peter, Tom and John who won the clean milk competition at East End Farm. It was sponsored by the Dairy Farmer newspaper

The horse that threw me off at ast End Farm 1935. The Lag is now part of M Alford's Park called Stoney Wish and has been beautifully landscaped

The author at East End Farm. "I always rode cart horses, though this one was not an easy ride"

Hassocks Station – Mr Jiles Edie (Catchpole). Notice the old cattle sidings are in the
background

is plenty of room and our housekeeper Lucy would look after you." I
agreed to remain at home for the time being to see how things worked out.

The following Monday I made a start. I had not been out of work a day
and yet in just under eighteen months I was starting my fourth job. As usual
I settled in quickly and could hold my place with most at hand milking and
soon got on in good terms with the other workers. When there was time to
spare and the cow stall work was done I used to go out onto the land for an
hour or so to help out. One day I was sent out to the front meadow to do
'thistle dodging' in the corn. We used a long push hoe with a small, sharp,
flat head and I walked up and down the field cutting the thistles just below
ground level. It was a lousy job, or at least that is what I felt about it. The
sun was hot and after a while I decided to have a break. I sat down under the
hedge and had a drink of cold tea, which most of the workers in the fields
would carry. I must have dropped off to sleep for the next thing I knew Mr
Muggerige was waking me saying, "John! It's twelve thirty, how about your
dinner?" I got up feeling guilty and we made our way together to the farm.
Whilst we were walking Mr Muggeridge said, "I wish you would come and
live in, my boy and have your meals properly." I did not reply at once then I
said, "I wish I could live in that caravan." I popped round to the buildings
and started eating my sandwiches with more cold tea. Soon it was time to
get the cows up for milking from the field. This was routine in the summer
months.

The sales of cows, batches of young stock, in calf cows and heifers were

My old railway carriage at Court Gardens drawn by Andrew Stenning

exceptionally good which meant Mr Muggeridge was often away buying in new stock to replace those that were sold. Mostly, replacements came from the West Country. Sometimes his trips would be for four or five days. He was always very fair in his dealings. He would always say to purchasers, "If you don't like them when you get them home send them back." There was very little bother.

When the cattle arrived at the railway siding at Hassocks station it was 'all hands on deck' to get them home. Before we moved them onto the road they were left to settle and were given food and water. During that time if any were a little overstocked with milk we would put a halter on them and ease them out as the governor would not have any sort of discomfort to any of his animals. One day, out of the blue, he came up to me into the cow stall saying, "Come up to the office for a moment, I would like to have a chat." On arrival he said, "I've been thinking about the caravan and although I would rather you came into the house to live you can live in the railway carriage. If it doesn't work out you can come into the farm house. The outside toilet will be available to you and our housekeeper, Lucy, will provide your Sunday dinner each week and anything else we can help you with." I was delighted and thanked him.

Soon my friend, Alfred came up and together we set to and gave it a jolly good spring clean. When it had got properly dried out we added a little paint. I purchased a few bits of furniture I needed and Mr Muggeridge came round chuckling and said, "That doesn't look too bad." I then went home. Strangely enough the next morning a dispute arose and I told my father I had made up my mind to leave home to look after myself. He told me that if that was what I wanted to do, it was up to me. I proceeded to put together my few belongings and off I went. I soon settled down to a plan and made up my mind to do my best.

I used to spend quite a lot of time, when the opportunity arose, to spar with a young man in the village called Ron Evans. He was a big fellow and about three years older than myself. He went into the R.A.F. as a flight engineer which unfortunately cost him his life. The strange coincidence about us was that we both won cups for boxing in the R.A.F., although at different times and at different stations.

My insurance man, Mr Bob Mayston, always used to be kind and have a chat. Often he would say, "Johnny you didn't ought to be living like this. I'm sure your Dad would rather you were at home." I just jogged on.

I was happy with my job and surroundings and I used to get a few games of cricket with Mr Kennings Lodge Hill X1, some evening matches at Ditchling and very occasionally football matches. I had also joined the Burgess Hill Boxing Club. It was run by Mr King senior and his son Steve. I was then nearing seventeen. Mr King was the landlord of the Cricketers Inn and the training was done in one of the out buildings. Gloves and a punch bag were provided and I found it quite a good activity. One person I remember was Mr Rumble. He was good and also a very hard puncher. Before we boxed it was agreed we done two rounds of sparring and in the third we were to put a bit more into it. The great thing with both Steve and his father was they never let anyone take too much. They would soon stop it if things became uneven.

* * *

When I was just seventeen I went to the fair on Lindfield Common. For a bet I went into the boxing booth. My opponent called himself 'Siki'. I survived the three rounds and received three pounds from the boxing booth and also won my bet.

As agreed I went to help out at East End Farm in the evenings. They kept their word and gave me driving lessons. It was not long before it was suggested I put in for my driving test. I did so, receiving quite a quick reply to go to Lewes. Unfortunately three days before the test the old Morris I had had my lessons in, broke down. It was too costly to be repaired and it was difficult to get another car. I ended up going to Garnet Grinstead, the owner of Keymer Garage. As I had very little spare money I made arrangements for a two hour lesson. Mr Grinstead provided his old gate change Austin Seven and it also covered the cost of him taking me for the test. It was a very difficult car to drive. The clutch was so 'sharp'. On my first attempt at driving it the car would shudder and just stop. This was repeated several times. The gearbox was very awkward as well and I used to crash the gears, much to the annoyance of Garnet the owner. He said, "You have no chance of passing your test and you should take more driving lessons." Again on the morning of the test Mr Grinstead was speaking as if I had already failed instead of giving me encouragement. After a crashing of the gears and a bouncy start we proceeded to Lewes. I am sure the driving tests then could not be compared with those of today. Lewes was considered to be a difficult place to drive at that time and there were many who failed. After making myself known to the examiner, I made a steady start and appeared to be getting on well. I took off on School Hill without dropping back and my confidence began to grow. I had slight difficulties with the three point turn as reverse gear was hard to find. The traffic built up so quickly I almost touched the curb. Finally I was told to pull in to the side of the road and was tested on the highway code. To my surprise and delight the examiner said I was safe and passed me. We drove home in silence. Mr Grinstead was furious after all the bad remarks he had made. Driving certainly stood me in good stead later on.

The days and weeks went by and business was good for the farm. I was still happy and in a learning situation, eating and sleeping well and enjoying sports whenever possible. I often saw my father in the village. We always stopped for a chat. "You seem to be managing very well," he said, "But should you wish, you would always be welcomed at home." I still continued to help my father with anything on the farm such as calving a cow. One year I thatched his stack for him. It was not a show piece but it kept out the wet and as I said I was still learning. If I arrived back at my caravan late at night and five in the morning was not too far away, I would change into my working clothes and go and sleep in the hay barn, near the cow stall, all ready for work. It was lovely and warm. I certainly lived well, Bladebone or Rump Steak with plenty of onions. I often made a good, big stew to last me two days, with plenty of vegetables. My favourite vegetable was swede. There were plenty grown on the farm for the cattle plus mangolds and kale and in the spring, a good crop of green meat Lucerne and other quick growing grasses. This was one of the cows favourite feeds, they certainly liked it.

My cooking was done off an old 'lean-to' off the cart shed. While the others were letting the cows out during the spring or summer, I would hurriedly light my fire and put my porridge on. I then ran round to drive the cows out to the fields to graze. I often had to put up with burnt porridge. I admit I used to hurry the animals to get back before my fire went out or my porridge was burnt. George the foreman used to grumble at me for this although at heart he was a kind man.

On one particular morning when I passed his cartlodge head quarters, I could hear him shouting and swearing about me hustling and hurrying the cows. As I got level with the cart lodge I turned to George and really let go at him. With a parting shot I said, "I have to get my own breakfast, you don't!"

When I returned to my porridge, George was there. He had made up my fire and was giving my porridge a stir. Handing me the spoon he said quietly, "That will give you a lift Johnny."

I replied, "Thank you very much." George was a wonderful foreman, a complete master of his trade and the farm's requirements. Mr Muggeridge would often have 'words' with him, yet he would always say, "Old George knows, you know. I don't know what we would do without him." I greatly respected him and learnt a lot from him. He done some fencing in the evenings

The NAAFI wagon at the RAF camp at Gatwick

for my father and he told me laughingly, " I told your old man I was keeping an eye on his prodigal son for him and that you look after yourself very well."

At Court Gardens it was the first time I saw and helped with a stationary baler. The made hay was brought to the baler by a sweep. This was farm machinery that pushed the hay to the stack to save loading it on wagons. We fed the hay into this stationary baler which baled the hay and tied it with a strong wire. This operation saved lots of time, although it was costly. It was the start of easier haymaking.

About this time the governor took on quite a lot of hill ground opposite the Goat, at Streat. It was an excellent place for stores. It meant driving them backwards and forwards I often went with the governor in the car to look at them. One day George the foreman said "I want you to help tie up the corn today." (That was just making sheaves round the outside of the cornfield so the binder could get in.) "I don't want you to go under the hedge for a 'MIKE'", he laughed. The governor told me all about that.

Later, whilst working in the fields, I remember watching a plane flying very low and it seemed to disappear behind the row of houses called the Waterman's Homes. Then there was a thud and the plane came down. I soon located the aircraft, which was a Fairy Battle still on the secret list at the time and it had come from Abingdon. There were two occupants, who apart from being shaken were unhurt. The police were there very quickly and later that day RAF Ground Staff took over. It had landed in the hedge of a small field which was owned by Alan Carter. The next field to it was farmed by Mr J Holman. The Fairy Battle aircraft were used later during the Second World War but mostly for reconnaissance because by that time superior aircraft had been produced.

Mr Wetz who owned Court Gardens Farm lived at Birch Wood, a large dwelling in Burgess Hill. He also owned a smaller farm which was called One O'Clock Farm. I only met the gentleman once to speak to. It was a summer evening. Mr Wetz and Mr Muggeridge were returning from a farm walk at Court Gardens Farm and I was doing some washing outside my caravan when they both came up. We had a laugh and a chat. Mr Wetz asked if he could look inside the van. Naturally I obliged and they both said everything was in good order and I appeared to be looking after myself well. Before parting Mr Wetz handed me a ten shilling note which I gratefully appreciated.

Although the farm was entered for competitions, we never seemed to get a top prize. It was difficult to understand. The herd was up to scratch, the milking was done under the strictest clean milk conditions, the cows were washed and groomed every afternoon and the foremilk taken with a strip cup. The dairy was excellent and clean, with pasture arable land and hedges kept in good order.

George the Foreman kept hedges and fences perfectly and any repairs needed to outbuildings were promptly and properly done. With the apples from the orchard all the farm's haymaking and harvesting cider was made and what strong stuff it was. I well remem.ber one hot day whilst haymaking, the cider frequently came out. The older hands were well used to it, however it began to take hold of me. I was glad when George suggested I went back to my van and have a lie down. I certainly enjoyed a good sleep. I woke at midnight and saw there was some cold steak and salad on the table with a nice drop of cold tea, it all went down well.

About that time Mr Hole, a farmer at Albourne won a farming competition. There was over a thousand entries by farmers and dairymen for the best commercial and hygienic methods of the production and distribution of milk. These frequent inspections, sample taking and recording of cattle all helped towards raising the standard and cleanliness of the milk supply. There were lots of good local farmers around at the time. Mr Hole was the starting of the real big milk business, Holes and Davigdoor, Southcoast and Unigate. All the smaller dairies were gradually taken over by them. Later I will be writing about the 'Ditchling Take Over'.

I worked with Mr Turner, at the time, and it was interesting how they did business. Another incident I remember was helping a farm worker at

Ann's sister Eileen who reached recruiting
sergeant in the ATS

John and Ann Stenning

Court Gardens, Bob Guy, lift a ten gallon churn full of milk onto the stand ready for milk collection. It was very cold and frosty and Bob said, "I can't get my finger out, it's caught under the churn." As I tipped the churn to release it the blood began to flow and on examination it was found that half of his finger was hanging by skin. He was hurried to the doctors but nothing could be done. After a few weeks he was back at work again and was able to carry on. When the stall was full we had as many as five hand milkers to cope with the morning milking. The farm had it's own water supply which was pumped into a large storage tank. This was another invention by George. I was getting along really well with him and he would sometimes bring me fish which a friend brought for his family and lovely new laid eggs.

The farm was trying to get self supporting with regard to food for the dairy herd. We grew more beans and peas for protein, oats and dredge corn (a mixture of corn seeds left over). More and more green meat was grown for the early feed in the spring to enable an earlier turn out of the animals that were kept in during the winter months. I began to thatch much more and I also learnt how to make my own thatching spars (splitting the hazels).

Friend 'Brummie' with the author during our training days – boxing, running, football, etc. He joined the RAF two months after me and died suddenly of a heart attack, aged 58

The country was now really threatened by war and for a couple of evenings I went up to the territorial hall in Haywards Heath. My pal Alfred and I had considered joining up. I mentioned it to Mr Muggeridge who told me he would probably be able to get me exempt, however that would have been the last thing I wanted. Soon after I was in Brighton and went to make a few enquiries in the RAF recruiting office. I almost settled and signed for a short period but my mind was not completely made up. I had a long chat with my friend Alfred and suggested we joined together, but he could not make up his mind and eventually joined up two months after me. In the mean time I had a letter from the RAF at Brighton suggesting I made the effort to see them because if I signed I would be most likely to get a job in the RAF to which I would be suited and happy doing. Later I called to see them suggesting I would like to be a PTI (Physical Training Instructor) as apart from work, all I wanted to do was take part in sport. I agreed to sign but was misled with regard to my trade. The RAF stated I would be sent for in about a months time. When I told Mr Muggeridge he was very upset. He did not want me to go and he would do his best to get me exempt should war start. I said it was too late now and I may be called within a month. I had a letter within a fortnight instructing me to report to RAF Cardington within fourteen days. A travel warrant was enclosed. The governor was very good to me when I showed him the letter and said I could have extra time off if there was any arrangements I wanted to make. As the day grew nearer he asked me in for tea and with his wife present we had a long conversation. They both wished me the very best of luck and told me to keep in touch. They invited me to go back to the farm for a third 'term' after if I wished to do so. I left my few bits of furniture in the van with a note attached saying 'To whoever it may concern'. The great day had arrived and I was off.

The camp I finally arrived at was RAF Debdon located near Saffron Walden. Airmen called it 'Debdon in the mud'. Several weeks of real tough training followed, marching, doubling, kit inspections and other inspections. Jokingly I sent a letter to the Muggeridges stating that I would be glad to return for a third term at the farm. I was really enjoying what I was doing. Strangely enough I did return to the farm later. I wrote to my family explaining my move and I was invited to stay for Christmas if I was given any leave. I was glad to accept.

One of our training sergeant's asked me to be his batman during my training stay. It meant a few privileges. He was a proper serviceman and he had seen lots of overseas service. He told me during a conversation not to volunteer for anything but put my name down for any sports should I be that way inclined. I did however volunteer for overseas but I found sports stood me in good stead. During my training interview I was informed that my application for PTI had been turned down. However as my education paper was satisfactory I was to be trained for an armourer. There was no choice but to accept. After basic training I was posted to No.1 Air Armament School situated at Manby in Lincolnshire. This I hated as there was so many technical sides that I was unable to grasp. This was such a difference to farm work. I was caught sleeping during one of our lectures. I was taken straight to see the training officer, F.O. Cleaver. The charge was read and I was asked for my comments. I pointed out that after being used to working in the open air on the farm I found it difficult to concentrate in the class-room. I assured him that I was doing my best. He was quite an understanding man. He gave me a good lecture and assured me that things would improve. He told me to carry on and try my hardest to pass and that he would take no action. He took a list of names from his desk and said, "I understand you're picked to play cricket tomorrow." I did pass the course with rather a low mark and was waiting to go on leave in the next few days but I had very little money.

My pal Alfred Brumsden, who was at the school, had the same time off as me. We borrowed cycles and went to a large fair at Grimsby which was twenty two miles away. At the fair in a large boxing booth I challenged

Mick Carney who was well known. We had four rounds for which if I survived I was to be paid six pounds. It was a good clean scrap. If I was still on my feet at the end of the four rounds I got the money. As it was such a good scrap the spectators started to throw money into the ring. The booth promoter had a collection to be shared by us both. I collected just over fourteen pounds. Alfred, whom I nicknamed 'Brummy' and myself stopped for a pint and then returned to the camp. The following day I went on leave to Ditchling, nursing a black eye and bruised ribs.

Having finished training I was posted to No.1 Squadron in Tangmere Hurricane Fighters. War was imminent and the day before declaration we moved to France, landing at Cherbourg. We went by sea on a boat called the 'Isle of Guernsey'. Unfortunately a small band of us fell sick after a short while and we were flown back to Tangmere. When I was fit again I did not return to France. I was posted to Tangmere. Things were beginning to get bad and I moved around quite a lot as I was so fed up. I decided to volunteer for overseas service.

I was posted to 22 Squadron at Northcoats and it was one of the worst incidents I experienced concerning a plane that we had loaded with bombs. Another armourer was fitting a flare but he should have looked to see the flare chute was closed. Unfortunately he had already attached the long and short static cord of the flare and of course, releasing the flair it started to activate. Naturally fire broke out on the plane. Several of us airman and the firefighters were at the scene. We were being sprayed by foam as we hurriedly debombed the aircraft. Everything was soon under control. Later all participants of this action went before the C.O. There were too many for awards but he congratulated us all on our prompt action. We had no trouble getting any clothing replaced that had been damaged. My next move was to Gatwick after passing a fitting armourer course in 1941.

After arriving, I was attached to the ground defence and for several days we used the ex-race course's stands as billets. Soon we were settled in a large house called 'High Trees'. I was in my element, playing cricket, football and hockey. I was able to pop to Ditchling often. There was an old farmer next door to the billets and he asked if any of us would help him with the haymaking. I had a few days off and built a haystack, at odd times I 'tucked the roof' and thatched it. This involved pulling the loose hay off the roof, which made a firmer base for laying the thatch. This was a good experience and the farmer and I remained quite friendly.

Whilst at Gatwick I was unlucky enough to be destroying some explosives. Instead of getting a delayed action I got an instantaneous action. Realising things were not quite right I put my arm up as a protection for my eyes and face. I was very badly burned and spent several weeks in hospital. My skin appeared to heal but my right arm was left bent with little movement. In spite of intensive therapy slow progress was being made. It was decided by the doctors I should go on three weeks leave and I was told to do my best to help my fingers and arm move. Whilst at home I started to try and milk an old Guernsey cow at my father's farm. Gradually the movement in both my arm and fingers showed improvement. On returning to sick quarters the doctors were really amazed with my progress. "What have you been doing?" they asked. when I told them the simple remedy I was sent for further home leave.

On being passed for duty I was sent on a short turret course. On returning and reaching London Underground there was a red alert and was told that there would be no further trains that night. There were lots of people camping for the night on the platform. I shall never forget a man's kindness who was there with his wife and two children. He could see I was wondering what was going to happen to me next. "You are not going to get any further tonight, come and kip down with us," he said. That was how friendship was. Frequently during the night tea was provided. I was also given a blanket. Early in the morning they gave me tea and sandwiches. I said my farewell with many thanks and I was off. I have never forgotten such kindness and shared hospitality.

Then in late 1941 I met Anastasia who was in the WAF at Gatwick. We got on so well we spent every moment we could get together. Ann came home to Ditchling and has liked it ever since. We married on 18th. March 1942. We got married by special licence and it was only a short leave. We had to laugh when we got back to Gatwick and told them of our marriage. We were immediately told we were supposed to have asked for the CO's permission to marry. We were so happy together and I dreaded the fact that my overseas posting would soon come through. A call from the Orderly Room told me I was not forgotten and I was to go on embarkation leave. I was to leave Gatwick in July 1942. The parting was awful when goodbyes were said but we both made up our minds and just hoped it would not be for too long.

When I arrived at the embarkation camp there was nothing doing for two or three weeks. I was wanting to make plans for Ann because there was a possibility our first baby had been conceived. In desperation I put in an application to see the CO requesting a few days compassionate leave for family reasons. A week went by and I heard nothing. I had a session of drinks in the naffi with a new acquaintance in the same billet as myself. He proved to be very down in the dumps for similar reason as myself. He said he had put in an application to see the CO several days before and like myself had got no reply. I said "I have put in to see the b*****d too and he won't see me."

Suddenly I heard, "AIRMAN COME HERE!" It was the station warrant officer. He took my name and number and told me to report immediately to the guardroom. "You will see the C.O., alright! I heard what you said." I was put on a charge for calling the C.O a B*****D. Sharp at nine in the morning I was marched into the C.O. LEFT, RIGHT, LEFT, RIGHT, RIGHT TURN. I was facing his desk but before I could say a word in front of him was my application form with 'Not granted' written on it. He told me it was a serious charge and he took a serious view of it.

"Have you anything to say?" I replied I was feeling depressed about my wife and had a few beers with a friend who was also anxious over a family matter. However I told him I was sorry. I had volunteered to go overseas and had made up my mind to go with a good heart but in this situation I could not care less what was to happen. Sarcastically he said "You will be going overseas and to ensure you do so you will report to the guard room every four hours until you leave this camp for embarkation. Right turn, left, right, left, right."

It was not long before we departed for embarkation. We were to travel on the 'Rankitiki' The boat was an Australian or New Zealand meat boat converted for troops. What a package! I was to share a table of six, I actually slept on the table. Hammocks hung everywhere. It was a large convoy and naturally at times we had aircover. A destroyer escort was always manoeuvring the ships moving a certain distance and then zig zagging.

After a couple of days out, the seas became very rough and choppy. As there was several cases of sickness there was lots of spare rations. After a few days the weather was gradually becoming warmer. Although we did not know it at the time we travelled out into the Atlantic and then made for Freetown our first stop. We were not allowed ashore but it was a bit of a respite. The natives kept coming round the boats to dive and catch coins and other small objects that were thrown to them. They were marvellous to watch and so active. Whilst we were at Freetown the German news agency reported the boat we had travelled on had been sunk. I read a plaque on the Rankitiki, it stated that her sister ship which was called the 'Rawpindi' was an armed merchantman protecting a convoy to Russia. When they came under attack from a German battle ship, the Rawpindi drew the enemy fire, although considerably outgunned. This enabled the other ships to scatter, many of which managed to reach safety.

Soon we resumed our journey. If we wanted we could sleep on a lower deck but it was risky. The decks were hosed down very early and if you were not quick all the bedding you possessed would get soaked. Daily we passed the time walking round the decks. There were several groups playing cards and some played bingo. Sometimes there was lectures and also plenty of boat drills for emergency situations. On Sundays we could attend an hour long service on the top deck in the officers' lounge. This proved very popular, not principally for the service although the parson always made us welcome and gave an interesting sermon the main reason for the large attendance was the fact that it enabled us to sit down and relax in very comfortable quarters.

After a few weeks we reached Capetown where our stay was to be for only three or four days. As a friend and I were leaving the dock we were approached by a very nice gentleman. Smiling, he said, "Hello! I'm sure you have had a long journey, how about coming with me to meet my wife and family, where you can have a bath or a shower and something to eat?" He introduced himself as Mr Purkiss. His family before him had settled in South Africa. We both thanked him and said we would be pleased to accept his kind offer. We got into his waiting car and were driven a short distance outside Capetown to Epping Garden village. This was a lovely spot. We soon met his wife and two young children who all gave us a wonderful reception. We had a shower while his wife prepared a lovely meal which we enjoyed with a few drinks. When they found out we did not need to return to the ship until midnight (it was then only early afternoon), it was suggested they took us over Table Mountain. What a beautiful trip. They invited us to get in touch if we were ever out again. We talked about our wives and families in England and asked for their addresses. Ann, my wife, received some lovely gifts from them.

Two days later we set off for Durban, where on arrival we were greeted by the deep voice of 'The Lady in White'. Apparently she welcomed all troopers with songs like 'There will always be an England'. She certainly was a true patriot. After a few weeks stay at Clairwood Camp we were strangely taken by the liner Aronsay back round the Cape to Capetown. The Aronsay was a very fast, comfortable transport and we were not in convoy. From the Aronsay we boarded the Fanconia which was not overcrowded. We were not allowed ashore and soon we were on our way again. The invasion of Malagascar was on at the time. The weather was lovely. The only real drawback was I had had no news from Anastasia. It was going to be a few weeks yet before I heard the good news but it was as we thought. She was expecting our first baby. I kept longing for the day when we would be back together.

The journey to India proved uneventful, just daily routine and trying to relax. Eventually we arrived at Bombay but after a short stay we started on a long train journey to Southern India (Madras Presidency). We were to reform 36 Squadron Wellington torpedo bombers. The squadron had been lost in the fighting in Singapore and we came under coastal command. Our huts had been constructed on what appeared to be a volcanic site. They were made of woven grass and bamboo and were quite comfortable. There was quite a panic when a creature was heard running about in the roof. This caused one or two sleepless nights. Jock Ferguson, a crack shot, soon put an end to it. The natives were exceedingly poor, hungry and primitive. They done their 'Dobie' (washing) in a large lake near the camp. As the photographs show the road construction was carried out by the women carrying the stones to the required place in a basket, which they carried on their head. A small grit like substance was put on the top and levelled. It was then wetted and they all sang as they pulled a large roller to form a settled surface.

The squadron soon became operational and by that time I had a good job tractor driving. This involved pulling several bomb trollies to and from the store, to the aircraft at dispersal. I made a trip to Trichinopaly to box. I did not make the finals but it was an enjoyable break. The squadron challenged the local police football team to a match. The visitors turned out without football

The first photo of Anastasia and Hedley in India

boots and gave us the runaround by winning five-two. We were stung by that and in a rematch, after a struggle we managed to draw. In the village was a little cafe called the 'Victory Cafe' where we were allowed to visit. There was also a small local church which had been recently built. We also discovered the graves of some early English settlers of the famous East Indian company. The 'charwoller' (tea) was always on hand and most of us could afford to have a bearer. They were very loyal and glad to get the money however small. They would clean your shoes, make your bed, or run an errand. The mail was arriving frequently and I was happy to learn Ann was settled and living with Doris, my eldest sister. Everything health wise was going well. I rarely missed a day sending her letters. Small detachments were made by the squadron to Colombo and also to the north of India.

Just as we were well settled the message came to make a departure. After a very long train journey we arrived at Dubulia, a large aerodrome and camp area. There was a small place near the camp called Christnagar, where I was surprised to find the Salvation Army. They were wonderful and I must reflect the many places I visited the Salvation Army were represented. The nearest large town was Calcutta. I went there once but it was not for me.

77

Things were hotting up so we did not leave camp much and the squadron was fully operational. Soon the good news arrived. I received an airgraph photograph of Anastasia and our new born son, Hedley, stating that everything was alright. Of course this increased my longing to get home but that looked a long time off. There was very little time for sport. However on the squadron there were two very good masters offering their education services. I was one of a few who took up their offer. It was to make a big difference to me and I settled down to improve my education in leaps and bounds. It was a great help to me later.

Our stay in our new surroundings lasted for several months and again we were told to pack and we arrived at Bombay. There we boarded the 'Amanzora' bound for Cairo. It proved to be a lovely trip. We had much more room and much better facilities than the early part of our travels. Soon we arrived at a large camp on the outskirts of Cairo and our troops had made such swift advances, everyone was really surprised. Of course the Pyramids and the Sphinx were visited. One day a friend and I decided to visit Cairo. I suddenly realised after we had spent some time walking around that we had strayed into an out-of-bounds area. Then a young boot boy threw some polish on my pal's shoe. He did not realise where we were and angrily tried to hit the young offender saying, "Wipe that bloody stuff off!" The boy gave a loud whistle and within seconds men and boys were running towards us in all directions. My friend looked very uncomfortable.

"Can you run?" I said, "Because you'll have to now." I remembered exactly where we had to get to. Luckily we were soon in a safe area but it could have been different.

After a short stay we were to go by land, all along the coast road to Algeria. I was lucky and got a relief driver's job in convoy. It was to take many days. We saw the remnants of the battles and one mountain pass that had blown up by retreating Germans. Due to it's importance it had been rebuilt by allied engineers in a matter of days. It was still very dangerous. We could see the vehicles down in the valley that had missed the bends. Suddenly coming round a pass we could see a lovely, green oasis. It proved to be the small town of Derna. We were not allowed to stop, only at recognised places en route. It was a wonderful but sad trip, seeing all the wrecked tanks and other equipment. Also the graves of the fallen friend and foe, marked with a plain wooden cross.

We arrived at Blida airport which was a few miles from Algiers. There were a few brick buildings which were used mostly by the Americans. We had a tented camp. It was very good and I thought, quite comfortable. All the action seemed to be over so we were once more kicking over our heels. There was plenty of sport. I was lucky and played lots of football. The North African Athletic Services Championships came up. We only had a

January 1942

Char wolla, India 1942

September 1939. Imchans, the
lake where they washed

1942, Dubalia, 15 miles from Calcutta

India 1942. Our hut

Left:
December 1942, India. The
camp and cattle at Vallum

79

In India with friends. The schoolmaster on the right gave me valuable lessons

very small squad but we were allowed to dotwo weeks full time training.
We had a PTI to help us and special food. The meeting was held at Algiers
stadium and lasted four days. The distances were all in meters and I was
entered in the hundred and four hundred meters. The standards were high
but 'I managed to get through the preliminary rounds in both. The
Americans and French had much larger and stronger contingents. However
on the Friday I was knocked out of the four hundred meters by an American
in the semi finals. I was still in the final heats of the hundred meters in
which I was beaten by a Frenchman. There were lots of servicemen at the
stadium as spectators. I was very pleased with what I had done. A notice
was put on our DRO's (Daily routine orders) congratulating our entries. It
was considered a good performance considering entrants did not all have
spikes and also the preparations were hurried, but there were some useful
performers.

The war news continued to be good and everything from home suggested
Ann was, like myself, longing to meet again. It was now over two years
since we had parted. The weeks went by but we had little or nothing to do
and everyone began to talk about the next move being home. Myself and
several others in the unit went down with Sandfly Fever. I felt rough for a
few days but soon recovered in the tented sick bay. A rumour went around
that there was another move coming. This proved to be correct as within a

Mosquito nets in the hut in India 1941-42

Shot by armourer 'Jock' Ferguson on the roof of our hut at Vallum in 1942

My brother, Dennis, in 1943 with the army in Tunisia

Final heats at Algiers. I came second after very little training

Above: The crowd in the station at Algiers

Left: I won the 100, 220 and 440 yards at RAF Station Blida, 20 miles from Algiers

Tented camps NA Blida RAF

My brothers Gordon and Dennis along with George Blackstone, who all met in Italy

A very good RAF side which included five professionals

A pile of old boots after a clothing exchange

The Western Desert

Anastasia

few weeks we were in Naples. What poverty, the war had left a nasty scar.

Now it was just like a long holiday. We were billeted near Vesuvius which had until recently been erupting. News came through that an advance party was named from the squadron to leave for England. I was lucky enough to be on it. We flew home in an old American Dakota which proved

Grave yard on the coast road

The author in Naples with Vesuvius in the background

85

8036 Echelon, Benbecula June 1945

to be a bumpy ride. We ended up in North Devon. There we had to wait and kick our heels for the remaining sea party to catch up with us.

However it was not to be 'home sweet home' for when the squadron was reunited we were moved lock, stock and barrel to the Outer Hebrides (Benbecula). Naturally I sent on the news that I was in England and looked forward to getting home as soon as possible. It was a further few months before I got leave. We had little to do in the way of work but we enjoyed football and other sports. Eggs were plentiful on the island and we used to pack five or six dozen eggs at a time in old petrol or oil cans and send them home. The crofters had a ready market. The cans were lined with cardboard, making very strong egg trays and in this way most of the eggs arrived in tact, with very few being cracked or broken. We had a sports meeting to which the crofters and the other squadron were invited to take part. Officers and aircrew made a book and I went off on the odds of two to one, in the hundred yards and landed a bob or two for the section and myself for winning it.

When coming home on leave from the camp, anyone who came from the South of England was flown to the mainland to reduce the travelling time. Demob was to be started soon and myself and a friend in the armament section were posted to Thorney Island, from where I could get home often. Everyone by now was speaking about demob but during that summer at Thorney Island the station sports were held. Yet again I had the good fortune to win the 220 and 440 yards.

It was advertised on the station notice board that anyone with an agricul-

WELCOME
HOME

1939 ~ 45

DITCHLING

WESTMESTON

STREAT

Ditchling, Streat and Westmeston request the pleasure of your company at a Welcome Home Dinner in honour of those men and women of the Villages who served in H. M. Forces and in the Land Army.

on Saturday, 7th December, 1946

at 6.30 p.m.

in THE SCHOOL ROOM, Ditchling

Please Reply

Miss Ellis
North Cottage
Ditchling

The dew pond where the drag hunt ran

The panormaic view from Ditchling Beacon

tural background who could find a farmer who would give them harvest work for six weeks, could apply. Naturally I was interested and Harry Guy, who was at Hayleigh Farm in Streat, was needing assistance. He wrote straight away for my six weeks release. I was over the moon about it. Working on the farm was several German prisoners of war, all, with a few exceptions, were grand people. Although they knew I had been on the opposite side they were very friendly with the exception of one. He was a real Hitlerite. He would not work, was a general nuisance and was soon got rid of. Harry Guy would bring us out some beer, bread and cheese and we all sat down together and enjoyed it.

After three weeks a telegram arrived from Thorney Island RAF camp requesting that I returned to run in interservice sports for the group. I was so happy to be home that I told them I was not fit enough and had had a slight accident whilst working. Of course the Japanese war had not ended but people were beginning to be demobbed from the service. It was not far away because I was actually demobbed on 6th December 1945. What a lovely Christmas present.

Although we were extremely happy Ann and I had no real money. My demob payment was just over eighty pounds. We also had to look for somewhere to live. This was proving very difficult. There seemed to be nowhere. I passed an entrance exam to take a resettlement course at Plumpton Agricultural College but would have to remain in the forces waiting for it to come through. That I was not prepared to do, although looking back it may have paid dividends. I started to have a good look round for work. I may have got back the job I left when I joined the RAF but I did not want anyone to be displaced on my account at Court Gardens Farm. I went to see one or two farm jobs but either house or job were not suitable. Ann and I were anxious to get a house other than a tied cottage and settle in Ditchling.

After a few weeks I heard of a job in Burgess Hill. I went down to meet the owner of West End Farm, Mr Marsh. We were offered a nice tied bungalow with the job. There was very little time off and the wages were a little above the minimum. We were to take charge of eighty to one hundred cows and followers. Milking was sharp at five o'clock in the morning and I knew it would be difficult but I had to make a start so I agreed. It was a good learning situation because the governor was a dealer. I done my very best but there were few workers that settled there and from the start I knew it would not be long before I would move on. After a few months, Ann conceived our second child. Where we were living was so handy for us as my sister Doris would help out at any time. Ann and Doris were great friends. Doris loved children but unfortunately had none of her own. We were always short handed as workers would get fired for just next to nothing on the farm. One day after several infringements and extra work I told the gov-

The Sandrock Inn darts team – three times winners in consecutive years in the 1950s

I won the ¼ mile cup for the third year running

91

Chailey Rural District Council

Housing

R. O. DALLAWAY
RATING
HOUSING MANAGER.
TELEPHONE: LEWES 1190

ROD/JMB.   18th January, 1951.

Dear Sir,

11. Southview, Ditchling.

I have to inform you that at today's meeting of the Housing Sub-Committee you were selected the Tenant of the above house.

This tenancy is offered to you subject to you taking Mr. Hills as a lodger. Will you please write to me and confirm that this condition is acceptable to you.

The rent is 15/10d a week exclusive and the rates amount to 6/9d, making a total of £1. 2. 7. a week.

You may move in as soon as Mr. Hills has made arrangements about his furniture and be is paying the rent up to the time you move in. Will you therefore let me know the date you propose taking over the tenancy and I will prepare the necessary Tenancy Agreements for you to sign.

Yours faithfully,

Housing Manager.

Mr. J.H. Stenning,
Caravan, c/o Elphicks Farm,
DITCHLING.

ernor I had thought things over and intended to look for alternative employment and should he find someone more suitable I told him to take them on. However on the following Saturday he said, "You are not going to work for me much longer John are you?" I had told him the position in good faith earlier in the week. "RIGHT!" he stormed, "You take a weeks notice and I shall want you out of the bungalow a week later."

I said, "Thank you very much." It was the only time I had ever had the sack. "I can get another job but I haven't got a house." "Where are you going to live then?" he asked.

"In your bungalow," I replied, "until you can get me out." As Ann was expecting we were allowed to remain in the bungalow for the three months before the birth and three months after. I had another job to start straight away but we remained in the bungalow for nearly six months. I went down

The author at Briggs Farm, Streat

to see Mr Marsh the evening before we were to move and told him to check that everything was left to his liking.

"John!" he said, "You bring me down that key and everything will be alright." We shook hands and wished one another well. We were back at Ditchling, well Streat really, which was quite close. Providing I played cricket for Westmeston and Streat, I was free to play football for Ditchling. It was hard going having to go back afterwards and work. I well remember playing football against Chailey. The changing room was at the pub 'The Horns Lodge' and we trotted round to the playing field which was near 'The Hook'. It was a drenching wet day and the scrub down was in cold water and then back to work for a few hours.

Whilst at Hayleigh we had the last addition to the family, Alan is now 50 years old. As it proved I was to go back for the third time to Court Gardens Farm, Ditchling. When I returned my old railway carriage was still there and was being used as a store. Ann and I were very happy about the move and I was over thirty and still enjoying sport. I entered the police sports held at Haywards Heath, finishing third in both the one hundred yards and two twenty finals. I managed to win the one hundred yards and quarter of a mile cups at Ditchling, each for three consecutive years. I did represent the one hundred yards trophy which was originally given to Sports Association by

Pouchlands Hospital. I received the Tutor's
Prize at the prize giving

Reverend Williams. Darts was a principal in sport in Ditchling and I was fortunate to play in the teams from the Sandrock Inn which won the league for three years running. Cecil Evans the landlord informed me, quite correctly, had I won my final match the fourth year we would have won the cup again. I was lucky enough to be in ten singles and doubles finals, having three wins and seven times runner up. However there has to be a loser!

We were happy at Court Gardens for the next few years and really it was a good life. Machine milking had taken over and lots of the hard labour was taken out of the work. However Mr Muggeridge was no longer young and he suffered lots of pain. This was due to an old but bad fall from a horse in his younger days. The farm and particularly the herd was going downhill and the owner no longer appeared interested. There was always an understandable threat of a complete change there.

There was one good story which caused a laugh. The governor had a few hens that used to roam around and lay their eggs wherever they pleased but the boss did not think that he was getting all that had been laid. However an egg was found in a nest in the hay and written on it was 'Thou shalt not steal'. Underneath it one of the lads wrote 'Lead us not into temptation' and replaced it. A few days later the chickens were cackling and there must have been more eggs Mr Muggeridge came into the cowstall with three eggs including the inscribed one. He was smiling, "Now lads," he said, "Leave my eggs alone. They are mother's (Mrs Muggeridge) and my breakfast."

Another strange character was called George (not Foreman George). He was known as a 'real old soldier'. He was a farm labourer. He used to come to work with his lunch in a red handkerchief. It was normally tied to a stick which he rested on his shoulder. When he went back he used to put a few handfuls of corn for his chicken inside his handkerchief. One day I was in the office having a chat and who should walk by but George, with his handkerchief and his stick over his shoulder. Mr Muggeridge said to me smiling, "I hope George doesn't think that I believe he brings his lunch up here and then takes it home again, but don't say anything to him because as long as he only takes small quantities for his chicken it doesn't matter."

It was sad seeing the herd as it was, sales were not of the best so finance was poor and the governor's heath was worsening. No replacements were forthcoming but it was still a good job and we seemed settled. I used to pick up a sporting life paper every morning for a local gentleman. I put it in his front gate as I was passing. One particular morning he met me looking pretty straight. "If this horse doesn't win the Lincoln today John then I won't be wanting the paper for sometime," he said. He had been investing other people's money. Sure enough the horse lost and he had to go away for a few months. The irony of it was the next time the horse came out and ran in a good race, it won.

Another horsey story to tell was we were playing darts at Scaynes Hill and in the team for the opposition was a jockey called Kevin Gilsenan. He was a character and already before the match he had had a few drinks. He was making all the movements on how he was going to win on a horse he was riding for Mr Geering at Plumpton the following day. I managed to get to Plumpton. A gentleman well known in the village always got me a pass if I wanted one. He was also a member of our darts club at the Sandrock pub. I saw Kevin before the race and asked him if he was OK and whether he thought he would win. "I've got a thick head from last night," he said, "But the horse is alright." Soon they were off but I felt for sure he could not hold it because the horse went off as if it was anything but the three mile chase. I just do not know how he managed it, coming down the hill. He hit the fence and Kevin was desperately holding on around his neck. I thought he was sure to come off but somehow it was his day. With the last fence coming up he was still ten lengths clear. He just jumped the last fence and with the pack closing in on him he managed to win. Twenty to one was the returned price. That was his only ride for the day and when I met up with him nearly an hour after, he was still shaking but what a lovely broad grin he had. "Did you put a couple of bob on for me?" he asked. I assured him I did and handed him the money.

We were happy to be in Ditchling but I did not like going in the governor's car. His driving was not up to scratch. He was very deaf and he rarely changed gear. He was such a religious and friendly person. He always found the time to talk to Ann and the children whenever he was passing our cottage. With the bulls he was unafraid. Moscow, one of them, always looked for him, as he often gave him a knob of cake or scratched his head with his hand or walking stick. The cats always crowded round him as he always produced something for them from his waistcoat pocket. He called them his Kitsie Parkers. He also appeared with a jug of tea every morning and the afternoons that he was in. One particular week when the clocks went back I forgot to alter mine. When Sid arrived, a chap who worked with me, I was under pressure. We always have laughed about this. I was really nasty to him. I asked him what time he thought it was and as soon as he put me right about the clocks I was really apologetic. However it ended in a good laugh. Sid was a good fellow to work with. He was trained by Alan West, a very large company, to do a much better paid job with electricity. He had to leave due to his failing sight. He was always joking and the governor regarded him very highly because he had an excellent rapport with animals.

I was offered a very good job at Elphick's Farm which was about a mile up the road from us. The owners Mr and Mrs Pritchard were very nice people and the money offered was well over the odds, although I knew I would have to be working long hours. The Pritchards were famous for their show

96

Above: Ditchling footballers.
Winners of the Division II of the Mid-Wussex League 1936-37

Below: Ditchling football teamin the 1950s

jumpers, both were first class riders but Mr Pritchard dealt mostly with the training side of it and his wife did the riding. I sometimes helped to 'muck out'. After I had been there a while they had great success with a horse called Music Hall at a Brighton show. They won a prize of fifty pounds which was a large sum of money at the time. I received a good present out of it.

There was no house with this job and it was agreed we would live in a caravan until either a house became vacant or buildings could be altered to house us. By then our family had grown to three children, all boys. This was my best job so far and Ann was able to earn a little extra in the farmhouse. It was not long however before two health visitors were to call and they came straight to the caravan. Although surrounded by duck boarding the site was very wet indeed. They told us that they would not allow us to live there in those conditions. I informed them that we had been promised accommodation would be found for us as we both had served in the R.A.F.. So far the authorities had done nothing to help our situation and three years had passed. The solution remained with them. It was not long before the council house number 13 South View became vacant and we became the new tenants. The Pritchards very kindly offered to pay our rent which was 17s 3d at the time. Ann was overjoyed and said that if a mansion was built at the farm, making it a tied cottage, she would never agree to move into it. After many years when the Government allowed people to buy, we managed to secure our's at a very reasonable price and it is wonderful to think it is one's own. I do feel however that more Council Houses should have been built as replacements as in no way everyone will be able to buy their own property. We soon settled down well at the job and in the cottage.

At Elphick's several hunting people decided to organise their own drag hunt. A tame fox was secured and the urine saved and stored. I was asked to run the drag for them which I agreed to do. The hounds were all proper fox hounds, some which were unsuitable or were not needed by the real hunt. It was a great success although there was plenty of work put into it. Both the fox and the hounds had to be fed and cared for and of course trained and exercised. My part of the drag was to map out a nice long course which on the day I covered by dragging a cord with a rag attached soaked with the scent of the fox. There was quite a lot in it because I would lift the drag at times and also weaken the scent. I always carried an extra little bottle of foxes urine with me. One day the finish was at the top of the beacon. I had reached there in time to watch the hounds working and yelping in the fields below. At the finish there was always entrails or meat placed for the hounds to enjoy as their finishing meal.

The last drag run was enjoyed by all followers. It took place on Ditchling Beacon. It was a very clear day and I was asked to make the run a lot

Ditchling cricketers v Sussex
J Holman, A Frost, AK Wilson, Ted Witham, Fred Edwards, Bill Kenning, Guy
Thornton, G Anscombe, Bill Brown, G Thomas, A Turner

Sussex County side Umpires M Tate (left) and George Turner (right)

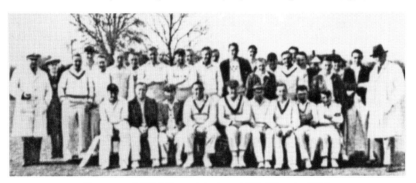

Sussex and Ditchling cricketers at Ditchling in 1935

Above: John and James Langridge at
Ditchling

Right: WL Kenning and John Dobson at
Ditchling Cricket Club pavilion

Below: 1 Jack Holman, 2 ? 3 Bill Hayston,
4 AK Wilson 5 E Withem, 6 F Edwards,
7 Guy Thornton, 8 ? 9 ? 10 Alf Turner
Bill Brown and G Thomas

longer. I set out in plenty of time and took lots of trouble to lay false trails and weak scent. From the finish I was able to enjoy watching proceedings, the huntsman jumping the Tiger Traps and the hounds giving tongue as they neared the end of the trail all ready to digest their meal of 'meat and lights'. Most of the horsemen and women agreed it was the best run they had enjoyed of them all.

Unfortunately Mr Pritchard was side lined for a while with a broken thigh but like all those tough horsey people he was soon back in the saddle again. My part of the drag was not a paid one but the 'cap' used to be passed round at the last meet of each season and I was handsomely rewarded.

Whilst working at Elphick's I was able to play cricket and football sometimes but it always meant returning to do the milking and bottle the milk. Whilst I used to sow the grass seed by a fiddle, although I learnt to sow quite well by hand and of course by then I could do the thatching. Having our own house separate from the farm I was free to do lots of odd contracting on my own, including digging foundations for houses. This was all hard graft but rewarding.

I left the farm and worked for a local dairyman. There were two principle dairies in the village and it meant I could start early and have half the day to do my other jobs. Soon however Mr Turner, my governor, had the offer of buying out the other dairy for a reasonable price. He suggested that I had a separate van and had my own round which I agreed to do. I done all the booking and bills for my part of the round and with the extra money for new trade, it was a good job.

After a couple of good, happy years, South Coast Dairies made their approach. At first it was turned down but those sort of people were not to be denied and another meeting was arranged. I must say that at that time Mr Turner's wife was in bad health and that I think, helped make up their minds to sell. I was asked by both sides to be there for the discussions. What astute men the South Coast representatives were. The first thing one of them done after introducing himself to me was handed me a five pound note and said," Put that in your 'sky rocket' (pocket) for your time in coming to the meeting."

In the end a deal was agreed. Mr Turner wished to take on a small, local part of deliveries and then return to the shop to enable help for Mrs Turner. Customers could still go into the shop and buy their normal dairy products and also pay their milk bill, if they wanted to. I was given quite a large round, and I was left to run it as I liked, within reason. It was agreed that I did not have to press the sale of dairy products to enable Mr Turner to carry on with his shop. They also allowed me a van, quite an old one but in good 'nick' which I was able to use for my own use if I wished. If we managed to keep all our customers for six months we were to receive a good present. This we managed to do. This arrangement concerning myself was to last eighteen months and then it would be revised. At that time we were already delivering the Sunday papers to Underhill Lane customers. They even allowed me to continue doing this, it kept customers happy.

At the end of the eighteen months a different arrangement was suggested. My pay was to be the norm for any roundsman and I had to sell dairy products on the round. This I did not really want to do and asked to do a different round away from the village? I was quite happy doing this.

Turner's wife was in bad health. I am sure this fact made them make up their minds to sell. I was asked by both sides to be there for the discussions. What astute men the South Coast's men were. After introducing himself, the first thing the general manager did was to hand me a £5 note saying, "Put that in your sky rocket (pocket), for your time spent in coming to the meeting."

In the end a deal was agreed. Mr Turner wished to take on a small local part of the round giving him more time and enabling him to help Mrs Turner. Cstomers could still go to the shop and buy their normal dairy produce and also pay their milk account if the wished. I took on a large round and was left to run it within reason as I liked and I did not have to push the sale of goods.

I was still interested in farming and I was trying to get bits of ground. In those days it was like gold dust. As luck would have it I was offered a small holding at Streat, a high ten year rental with an option to buy at the end of the tenancy. Unfortunately the same solicitor acted for both parties but in the end it was to become an embarrassment because as the years went by, difficulties arose. I had a lovely little herd there and I had to do lots of odd jobs to keep things going.

Mr Catermole from Haywards Heath market was a real friend to me. One day I was at a sale with no intention of buying and there was a nice Guernsey with her second calf in the ring, sent there by a local Young Farmers' Club. The bidding was slow because she was an animal that wanted making. However I was most surprised when the hammer fell it was knocked down to me. I anxiously looked towards Mr Catermole who winked. After the selling had ended I went straight round to meet a smiling Mr Catermole. I told him that I did not bid for that young cow because I did not have the money. He told me that he had realised that but he thought that I could do with her. The Young Farmers' Club wanted her to go somewhere, where she would be looked after in a small unit. I thanked him and settled my account in the following two months. The cow done me proud, Mr Catermole was that sort of person.

Another good dealer was Jack Speller from Plumpton. He often got me a

Above: The first railway
station at Burgess Hill

Right: The farmyard
that stood by Burgess
Hill railway station
many years ago

Below: An old view of
Church Road, Burgess
Hill

The handsome dark green Riley that Bill Kenning had from new in 1923 until his death in 1967

Hassocks railway station

cow or two on the understanding that he would take them back if they were not suitable. He always told me that he did not mind that agreement with me because the cows were always well fed and looked after and they would always be improved if he did take them back.

Already years before completion I had made arrangements with a bank so that I could exercise my option at any time should it arise. I managed to get a further eight acres but being a few miles away it was difficult to make

104

the maximum use of it. Soon a challenge came from the owners. Realising the weakness of having the same solicitors I immediately changed mine. A case was brought, which was at Brighton County Court, the presiding judge was well known in Sussex. I was being questioned about an agreement between myself and the Landlord by the opposing barrister. After answering a few of his questions he drew himself up to his full height sharply saying, "But he didn't say that did he?"

I replied to him, "I was there and you were not -What did he say?" The Q.C. looked as if he had been shot. The judge rapped on his bench and said, "Witness, you are there to answer questions not to ask them." The judge asked the barrister if he wanted to ask any more questions and he stated that he did not. The end of the matter was that the case was judged in my favour and I received fifty guineas costs.

The next thing to be brought was a land tribunal which states that no-one need not have solicitors unless they wished to do so. I think this is very stupid because the questions that were asked would have been very difficult to answer by a layman, like myself. At the same time it was taking any money I had and I had to sell off young stock to raise the cash. However I had done lots of improvements to enable me to get a milk licence. Again it was found in my favour.

The time now came for me to exercise my option to buy, but at the last moment because of the bad financial position of the country, banks were not allowed to advance the money. I received a letter to this effect. This was the last straw and when money was so difficult to obtain, what could I do? I sold my option for a very low figure and then once again the Landlords challenged the agreement and I just sat tight, both solicitors writing to one another. At the time I was doing odd garden work for the recorder of Nottingham. His wife explained it was difficult to catch him in the right mood when he was off duty. She suggested that when I came to work for him I should carry a copy of the agreement with me about which so much trouble had arisen. A few weeks passed and the solicitors were talking about going to the Chancery Court but I was nearly broke. As luck would have it I caught him on the right day and his wife took a copy of the agreement in for her husband to read. In less than half an hour he came out and told me that the agreement was completely water-tight. He advised me to return to my solicitor and request that he issued a writ and claim damages from them for not signing up. This was done and after several days my Landlord agreed to sign and to pay the damages and some of my costs. I did come out on the right side but the solicitors, by their piles of correspondence had the lion's share. However I sold up some of the animals and went as a night assistant at Pouchlands Hospital. I liked the job very much but staffing was bad. Many a night I looked after 64 patients, naturally I had help with the ones confined to wheelchairs and many residents helped one another. One night whilst on duty the nursing officer came round. He commented that everything seemed to run smoothly when I was on and he suggested that I went for training. As I was just over fifty I did not think I would be able to find a course that would accept me. The nursing officer said he would try and find something suitable. A few days later he brought me some papers to fill in and.on completion I had to get some character references. Several weeks later I had to go before a selection board and I was told straight at the interview that there was two main things against me becoming a nurse. These were my age and my education because I had to put Hassocks Council School. They told me that if I passed an entrance exam I could go forward. It was quite stiff really, the money was nothing so I had to do other jobs, when I could, to supplement my income. I did not have much money left after the farm finished. I gained my S.E.N. and a night duty job at Pouchlands. After another five years I gained Senior S.E.N. and enjoyed thirteen years at the hospital.

The training was done between four hospitals, Pouchlands, Chailey Heritage, Laughton Lodge and Hellingly. I thought the upbringing of mentally handicapped people had taken a big step forward. Originally there was the Ditchling Workhouse, Chailey Workhouse and Ringmer Workhouse. These places provided short stay accommodation and perhaps work to destitute people. Even whilst I was there I met one inmate and perhaps there were more, who were there during the second world war. I also met a mentally handicapped person who had helped the farmer on the small holding I had in Streat. Apparently the three were amalgamated to form the Chailey Union Workhouse. I read that in 1871 there had been 75 inmates at Chailey, 21 at Ringmer and 25 at Ditchling. A site in the village of East Chiltington was bought for a few hundred pounds and the workhouse was built for ten thousand pounds and the older ones closed.

I have read that picking oakum was a common task for paupers in work houses, as well as for convicted prisoners. This work entailed pulling the fibres loose from old ropes and these were used, amongst other things, with tar to stop up the seams of ships. Picking oakum was a painful task, tearing the skin on the hands. They were also made to break up flints for chicken farmers. These unpleasant tasks were stopped and the paupers were given outside work, tilling the soil and growing vegetables under supervision. In the old days of the workhouse, the bell was rung at intervals during the day, to wake the people (or paupers) in the morning and to call them for their meals. There was also a steady stream of migrant vagrants who moved on from workhouse to workhouse. Remember earlier I mentioned Mr Linsor at Gospels Farm. They were given lodgings for a night but they were locked in their rooms. If they had any money on them at all they were asked to contribute towards their stay. When leaving they were given a quantity of brewed tea and some bread for their journey, perhaps to the next work-house. Some of them got crafty and would hide their small amount away in the hedges before they entered. I am sure things must have been very bad. Male attendants looked after the male inmates. There was also a matron to care for the sick.

I knew a fellow for a number of years. He was there during the last war and he suffered from Scissor Gait (the legs cross and make it difficult to walk). When he was able to he used to wash down the concrete stairs. Later he had operations which I know helped him quite a lot. In 1947 when it was under the provisions of the National Health act it was renamed Pouchlands Hospital. It came under the administration of the Mid Sussex Management Committee, this was later changed to East Sussex Area Health Authority. After 1947 mentally handicapped patients were admitted for long term care and the casual wards for vagrants had ceased.

When I was at Pouchlands it was gradually being updated. Many alterations had and were being made. Pouchlands had approximately two hundred beds that were divided into two separate blocks. There was a wing for the long term care of geriatrics and also occupational and physiotherapy units. I done my training on course S.P.1. I was the first nurse to pass. The mentally handicapped wing included a pupil nurse training school and an in service training scheme for nursing auxiliaries. The League of Friends were very good and a little shop was provided. Also, at great cost, there was a recreational hall and a magnificent greenhouse. The gardeners worked hard and everything was kept up to scratch with lovely flower borders and lawns. There were also recreational facilities inside and out. There was a sports ground where everyone could enjoy the open air. Strangely, when I think, everything had improved. Lifts were installed, the wards were made smaller and carpeted. Houses or bungalows were built to encourage more staff and now it is all pulled to pieces. I also used to take the residents on some wonderful holidays and one felt they had done something. I also took them swimming to Chailey Heritage and ran a gardening group. As a matter of fact, when my heart problem started I collapsed in the greenhouse and they quickly ran over to summon some assistance from hospital staff.

I was retired at the age of sixty three, my working life was, by far, the best. I only wished I had turned to nursing much earlier in life.

I must not close without a word about Bill Kenning. I would think the first time I saw him was between three and a half to four years old. That was when Ditchling were using the Gospels to play their cricket. I am sure it was right to find somewhere different as Gospels was not suitable. We spent a few years at Hassocks, I was always in Ditchling and I followed all the local sport with interest. Bill Kenning was always friendly and he did his best to get me off work, for a game of cricket. He also persuaded me to go to the Ditchling Cricket dinner. I was fifteen. The Sussex Cricket Club were represented by Maurice Tate and Tich Cornford. Mr Knowles was there and other celebrities. Bill Kenning often came around the farms on which I was working when he was waging war on crows and magpies. He was responsible for bringing more and better players to the village. I remember when one of two of us would have to stand down when players from private schools came home for their Summer Holidays. I soon learned from them, being properly coached. There was the two Amores who were lovely people and brilliant fielders and then the late Tom Carson who got lots of runs and who used to dance down the wicket. I feel a sadness when I see the latest names on our War Memorial as I knew them all. I know many cricketers had differences with W.L.K. but the next time you met him he was the same friendly person. With his Lodge Hill team we played amongst many teams including Surrey Sevens and Watersfield. When I came home from the forces he was very helpful in us getting a Council house. I would have loved to enjoyed more cricket for Ditchling but I chose agriculture for a living and a means to bring up our family of three boys. Bill Kenning was a sport. On Wednesday football games we were always short of players, before the war. I remember him coming and playing. A few times and at the sports, if there were only a few runners for the mile race, he took part.

One morning I was cycling from Burgess Hill to Hayleigh Farm just after the war about five o'clock. As I passed the recreation ground Bill Kenning ran into the road and with arms outstretched said, "John! You are under citizen's arrest. I want you to help me move the roller." I explained that I had to be milking at 5:30 but he replied, "I'll tell Harry (my governor) when I see him if you are late." What a man, up at that time, preparing for the enjoyment of many. He used to give you a card telling you when and where you were picked to play cricket, adding his famous words, 'You have been warned!'. He had a large garden at Lodge Hill and when I had my small holding he wanted to fence it off to make extra grazing for young stock. It was a very kind thought but it was not practical to do. I had been delivering milk early in the morning and he would often come in from the garden to make tea and tell me of his day's plans. In the Summer it was usually cricket, train spotting or pest control. What a tragedy to happen to such a sportsman, to be hung up in an apple tree. He was certainly sadly missed. Over the years he had done so much for the cricket of Ditchling and Ditchling village. Reading a very old book called the Cradle of Cricket I came across the name of Borrower of Ditchling, who was said to be high quality as regards to cricket. I wonder if Barrons Platt in Ditchling could have been his abode. In St Margaret's churchyard there is a tomb with the name and a date of approximately his time as mentioned. There was also a person named

'Wood' who came from Ditchling, who played in very few matches but who was a very fast bowler. I was also told cricket was played on Ditchling Common. My father said he had seen matches played there.

One day I was at Mr George Leaney's house situated on Ditchling Common and he told me there was so many Leaney's about, he also mentioned cricket in Ditchling. In the corner of the room stood a cricket bat. George told me to pick it up and look at it. On picking it up I saw the words D.C.C.C. and a date early in the 1900's on it. I said, "That's not Ditchling Cricket Club!"

"No!" he told me proudly, "It's Ditchling Common Cricket Club." Every year a bat was given to the player with the best batting average. Apparently there were lots of cricketers from the brickyard. The wicket was situated between the Common road and the Common pond and lots of fun was had there. In 1989 a team of Scraces from Burgess Hill challenged eleven of the Leaneys from Ditchling Common. The sides were very well matched. The Leaneys won the game by one run. For a year or two matches were arranged by Mr Knowles and Mr Kenning, Ditchling v Sussex. I only had the good fortune to play in one game. Ditchling batted 18 and fielded eleven, however er lots of people turned up. As things progressed the wicket and out-field were greatly improved and the standard of teams became better and better. The Wednesday team fell by the way after several years but both Saturday teams seemed to prosper. The cricket week was quite an attraction and there was an extra boost when Sunday cricket was introduced. I played when I could and thoroughly enjoyed every minute of it.

In 1921 Fred Gearing, who was to become an uncle of ours, who lived opposite the Friars Oak public house, was courting our Aunt Annie. She lived and worked at a house several yards away called Clayton Priory. Uncle Fred left Hassocks Station in January 1921 to make his fortune in Australia. He was soon established and the following year he asked my Aunt to marry him. This she did in the Autumn of 1922 and when they came back and stayed with us, late in the 1940's, they told us plenty of interesting stories. They made their way in Australia for several years having obtained a holding which they farmed in Queensland. Then a bad drought hit them and they sold what they could and went to Tasmania. They settled at Glenorchy where they had a bungalow built and ran a progressive fruit farm. Later Uncle took a permanent job and reduced the One Man Business

They both told me stories of the old days at Hassocks. Uncle Fred said it was very hard working on the farm at Hassocks. Like myself he had to work all hours. He said he had read about the past and told me that Courts were held at the Mound at Ham Farm in Hassocks. The judges or magistrates were the landowners. The courts were held monthly but later many working people became thrifty and with the aid of Building Societies began to gain their independence and own their own property. Uncle told me that he left school at the age of twelve. It was surprising how he wrote things down and they both could work out L.S.D. He also told me he chorus of a song which was sung at the time.

> My glorious Sussex in thee I would be.
> I'd walk in the pastures and dream by the sea.
> I'd labour and love as the great breakers roll
> In Sussex, glorious Sussex.

Uncle Fred also mentioned about a stage coach stuck in the snow at Stonepound. The travellers and the horses had to seek refuge in the Friars Oak Inn. He said his father often took him to see the trains explaining the first were only open wagons, much to the travellers discomfort in bad weather.

Aunt Annie told me in the house called Clayton Priory, there were writings about the Priory which mentioned the Friars and the Monks who lived there. For many years they would sit under a large oak tree nearby, play music and sing. They gave medicine and food to the poor and needy, if they were brought to them or just passing by. Mr and Mrs Jupp, who kept the Friars Oak Inn for many years, up until the early thirties, were the parents of Vallance Jupp, the England cricketer. He also played for Sussex and Northampton as a county cricketer. I think he was born in Burgess Hill.

John Burgess, a Ditchling Diarist wrote he went to a "Bull Bait" at "Friars Oake" and there was plenty of wine and punch all afternoon and also a great many people. I understand a Bull Bait to be a type of Bull Terrier fighting dog with especially strong jaws. In those days owners and interested people used to love to watch them fight. Large amounts of money would change hands on "wagers" on the outcome of the fight.

Aunt Annie and Uncle Fred told us that if we were to go to Tasmania they would look after us until we got established and their property would be left in our favour. As we both quickly declined the offer, their home and land would go

Ted Waghorn and horse

110

DITCHLING FAIR

Top left:
Ted Waghorn (also the picture
beneath this)

Left:
'The Archers'
Frank Weller, Albert Holmes, Jean
Saunders, Charlie Saunders, Vera
Weller, Bert Sellens, Stan Faver, Alf
Smith, Bert Longley

Below:
Maypole dancing at Ditchling Court

111

DITCHLING FAIR

Bottom picture:
Harris's roundabouts in North Star
field ready for the flower show

112

to Trust - this , I imagine , is what happened. We were both content to stay in Ditchling.

It is written that there was a hailstorm in Sussex on August 29th 1763, some of the hailstones were like snowballs and lay over 1 foot deep.

In 1810 the first regular mail "horse coaches" were placed on the London to Brighton road, it was an eight hour journey. In 1882 forty two coaches were running daily.

My collection of cups and trophies

I have also read DITCHELLING Currant and Gooseberry show, Kettle feast and stoolball matches "founded". I attended the annual show for 35 years. Medals were struck for it; kettles were given as prizes and the stoolballers played on a show day. Stoolball was purely a Sussex game. It was originally played by milkmaids who used their three legged stools as bats. Years ago at the show a dozen. gooseberries weighed over 15ozs and were sold for 7d each. The Southdown band (Poynings), rendered sections of music playing to official Representatives dining at the Bull Hotel. Mr F.F. Wood was, for many years, Hon. Secretary of the show. He was a clever naturalist and author. He identified 108 species of birds, 400 moths and over 700 plants in Sussex. I remember the show there was always a great occasion. I myself can also remember the stoolball matches being played just above the tented area. The ladies of Ditchling always played stoolball at a very high standard.I have taken part in matches where the ladies played against the men. Doreen Mayston had the honour of representing the county and was a fine player.

Robert (Titch) Mayston, Doreen's late husband, left us far too early. He enjoyed all sports and was a tireless worker for the Ditchling Cricket Club. He used to make our evenings at darts~ For several Christmas's small gifts were distributed to every old age pensioner in the village. They were bought with money raised during the season. It was much appreciated by the old folk and the club received lots of nice letters of thanks. Titch was an excellent footballer and played for many years. The Ditchling football teams seemed to have good players and teams. Many matches were won and even a few cups. We had many good years. I first played in men's football at fifteen. These are football photographs of teams. The bad state of my legs now suggest I should not have played.

The Brighton Line was opened in 1840 and in 1933 the change from steam to electricity was completed. I remember at school we had a debate, which would be proved the best steam or electricity. It was just for a little interest, I suppose. Joy Sinden led the debate for electric trains, she was always very good at English.

Aunt Annie from Tasmania

A story I am going to mention has always been of interest to me. I have read another version of it. It is about a Gypsy called Matthews who had pitched his tent at the bottom of Ditchling Beacon, near Wick Farm. He left his wife and children to walk to Horsham. During the few days he was away there was very heavy snowfalls in the district. On returning, Matthews, although worn out after his long walk, searched everywhere to find the tent in which he had left his family including the dog. However the terrific snow falls had buried everything. Eventually he decided to move towards the farm yard whilst calling out his dog's name. Suddenly the dog, who must have heard his calls came bounding towards him. Matthews' dog barking excitedly, led him to a large barn where his family had taken shelter from the dreadful

Brighton 1968. Uncle Jack (Tasmania) with Ann and John Stenning

114

The construction of Balcombe tunnel

weather. They were then happily reunited. The picture of the barn is taken from a painting by a well known artist from Ditchling, Miss Rawlins.

In 1908 the parish council of Ditchling beat the boundaries of the parish, other people joined in, this exercise was done over two days. Apparently the Bounds had been "beaten" forty years before.

The first cricket match I put my name forward for when I arrived at R.A.F. Gatwick was played at Horley. Our captain was a tall elderly man, much too old to be playing cricket or so I thought. We had to field first. Our opponents were local. The captain who was keeping wicket eventually asked me to bowl. I had a fielder in close because one particular batsman was just poking about. I was also bowling a bit short hoping for a catch. Suddenly the captain shouted, "Stenning! Pitch 'em up." It seemed to echo around the ground and there was laughter. It was my intention for my next ball to be really pitched up. It seemed to slip out of my hand and went right over the batsman's head and rather wide of the wicket keeper. He made a desperate dive but the ball was already on it's way to the boundary. The captain waved his hands and said enough after the over was completed. Luckily I managed to get some runs when we batted. We were enjoying a little refreshment after stumps were drawn and the captain came up to me and said, "Stenning! Did you know I have captained Sussex?"

"No Sir," I replied, "I did not know that, but I have often been to the County ground."
"Next time you are at the pavilion look for H P Chaplin," he said. I told him I would. "I was pleased with your batting but your bowling was awful," he said. After the war I went to the Sussex County Ground and there in a photograph in the pavilion was H.P Chaplin, five years captain of Sussex - his top score was two hundred and thirteen in an innings. He also had an overall average per innings of twenty four. When he played the match he must have been fifty five years old and I was just over twenty - still it is only a game!

Ditchling fair is an exciting time for the village. It was also well patronised by many people outside the neighbourhood. An important character for a few years was Edward "Ted" Waghorn. He was a lovely, friendly person to know and a good family man. He was a carter by trade and he loved his horses. He also had a vegetable garden which was always kept very special. I met him frequently whilst he was enjoying his "pint". He had a slight foot deformity. He was a happy person. He would order his pint and take a seat. If the dart board was free it was not long before he would say, "What about a game of arrows?" "I can't score." he used to add. Ted was a good player and if during a game a mistake was made regarding the score, he would quickly say, "Come on, check that score!" On the great fair day he would dress up in his smock, have his horse prim and proper with glistening brasses, as the photograph depicts and he would take charge of the fair queen and her attendants during the parade.

I met Mr J.C. Bee Mason of Burgess Hill, a member of Shackleton's Artic expedition in 1921, an Oxford University Artic expedition in 1924, the British Artic Expedition in 1925 and also the Bolivian expedition in 1928-29. He used to lecture to large audiences all over the country. He took a great interest in bee keeping. Later he became rather eccentric (picture).

In 1921 there was the shock sudden death of Reverend Norton. I understand he baptised me. He was aged 73 and he was the village vicar for 38 years. Mr Norton was feeling unwell as he was returning from Brighton by motor car so he decided to call on Dr Eggar of Hassocks. There he collapsed and died almost immediately. When he came to Ditchling in 1883 he was greatly interested in the Chichester Men's Club which was then a flourishing institution in the village. He presented an organ to the parish church in memory of his mother and two of the bells in memory of his brothers. During the Great War, at his own expense, he rented two houses in East End Lane, for the use of a Red Cross hospital in which both his daughters worked. He also had a church room built and gave it to the church. It was the same church room where I attended my early Sunday School. The Reverend Norton also took a great interest in research work and excavation.

116

Ted Miles' Garage at Burgess Hill in 1900

Burgess Hill c1900-1910

117

Left: My sister Doris' husband as a post-
man in Burgess Hill
Above: Ben Mason of Burgess Hill
Below: Brother-in-law Fred about 1930

Ann's father with a nice salmon

Ann's mother

I first met Jack Weller when I went to help Harry Guy with the harvesting. I obtained Agricultural leave towards the end of the war. At the time he had made his home in the loft of one of Harry's buildings and so a little later after my demob I got to know him well when Ann I moved into a cottage on the farm. He was a real countryman. He kept himself clean, was able to do lots of knowledgeable jobs on the farm and he loved his little black dog named "nigger" who was his constant companion. He and Nigger would go out into a field or anywhere to work sometimes for many hours. He would just tell Nigger to "stay" and that is where he would remain.

I was told to go and help John who was thatching a large corn stack in the farm yard. As John was such a good thatcher he did not approve lightly of help. My particular job was to prepare and carry the straw up the ladder to the stack roof and leave it in a convenient position for Jack to lay it on the stack. I put a little extra into my preparation of the thatch and then carried it up to him. I could see by his manner he was displeased however I left him to examine it on the stack and descended the ladder. I then began preparing some more straw. Jack, meanwhile, was still looking at what I had taken up to him. "What do you expect me to do with this rubbishy lot?" he said. "I hoped you were going to put it on the stack," I replied. With that

Ote Hall Chapel, Wivelsfield. This has been altered since a car ran into it

he threw it all down to the ground. Of course we had a lively exchange and then he said, "I'll come down and show you how to prepare it properly." After lots of time I was asked to resume and we worked away well. The finished job was passed "first class". A couple of years later he was given a caravan and it was placed with a farmer for whom I helped out with milking.

Poor Jack had deteriorated and one day I found him with breathing difficulties. There was nothing for it but hospital, he was quite ill for several weeks. However when I went to see him in the ward the first thing he said was, "What did you bring me to this place for? I would have got well with Aspirin tablets." Ann, my wife, helped by straightening out his van ready for his return but he did not really express great appreciation. However we remained friends. Unfortunately he died at Uckfield. He was unable to care for himself but in his time he was a knowledgeable, warm, independent character.

I am sure many people must remember Richard, our happy go lucky son, who unfortunately got knocked down by a car just two hundred yards from our house. After 12.00 o'clock that night I was awakened by a policeman and I was taken down to the scene of the accident. Richard was training for a charity walk. He is still greatly missed by the family. He seemed to get along well with everyone and he spent several happy years working for the late Alan Oughton, a local racing trainer. He looked after one very good horse called Solymth who won several races. Richard loved leading him

The barn in which the Matthew family took shelter from the terrible snow storm

round the ring. Solymth ran in the Grand National but that, I think, was well beyond him. Had not Richard got so heavy I am sure he would have stayed in racing and working with horses as it was something he really enjoyed. Richard enjoyed a drink and a chat. He remained cheerful with plenty of friends until the end. They certainly all done him proud, giving him a lovely "send off". I am sure there was nothing more he would have liked. He could well be described as a countryman and a good companion. Richard R.I.P. aged 29 years.

My wife Anastasia, normally called Ann, was born at Kells, a tiny village in Southern Ireland. She was one of a large family. Her father, like mine, was a harnessmaker and he often worked away from home for days or even weeks at the many large stables in the area. He was also known as a good distance runner in the locality. Ann's mother, I am told was a lovely, little lady. Unfortunately I did not have the pleasure to meet either of Ann's parents. During the war we exchanged lots of letters and they were all very informative and reassuring to me, she felt sure Ann would be alright. The Hurleys lived near the famous Mount Juliet stud and stables owned by Major McCalmont. Whilst on holiday we were shown round by friends who knew them. I saw the tombstones of several great race horses and brood mares, amongst them the great Sceptre. Ann's schooling was similar to

121

Above: The Church of the Holy Cross, Kells in 1932. This is the village where my
wife Anastasia was born in a cottage in the road on the left

Below: Kells Cross in past times showing what is now O'Dwyer's shop, pub and
Kell's post office. Smith's Garage now stands on the site of Tobin's old house

mine, three teachers who certainly done a good job. When she became old enough she came to England and found work with a family. She used to send money back home to help her parents when she could afford it, likewise as did her sisters. Prior to joining the R.A.F. Ann had the bad experience of being bombed out whilst in London, but she says very little about it and it was not until recently I got to know about it. When war broke out she joined the W.R.A.F. and passed her catering course with L.A.C. marks – over eighty per cent. As I have stated I had difficulties to scrape through on my Fitt Arm Course with Ac. 2 marks.

Ann is an exceptional lady and has always done everything possible for the family and when differences arose she would take everything so calmly. During the war and when I was overseas we kept up a lovely correspondence and on my eventual return we started where we had left off. When in the end we got our council house No.13 South View, which is now our property, Ann stated that she would never want to move again. We had an allotment for over forty years and with the exception of potatoes, we were always self supporting, as well as giving vegetables away to family and friends who wanted them. On the last year we were able to do the allotment properly we won first prize of fifteen pounds for the best garden. We missed out on the cup which was given the following year.

Our eldest son Hedley's marriage produced three super grandchildren. Mark, the eldest, is unfortunately handicapped, but he is a lovely person and

A view of the 'V' and the chalk pit at Plumpton

123

My son, Richard at Odland Cottage, Keymer in the summer of 1975.
He was tragically killed in Common Lane on Ditchling Common at midnight on
29th May 1977

a joy to be with. Rachel, the next in line, is happily married to Peter with two lovely daughters. Rachel appeared very unlucky, as before her marriage spinal cancer was discovered from which she recovered. Unfortunately a year after her wedding, a second cancer appeared, but Rachel, a great fighter, was not to be denied and again recovered and has had the "all clear" for four years. She is now a very busy young mum with two daughters Jasmine aged 2 and Darcy 7 months at the

Richard on his favourite horse, Solimyth

124

time of writing. Rachel and
Peter seek nothing but the best
for the family. Andrew, my
third grandchild has just completed his university studies
successfully achieving his BA
(Hons) degree for which everyone is very proud, lets hope a
suitable job will now materi-
alise. Ann and I are very proud
of them all.

This little book is dedicated
to Ann and the family. I want
to point out how lucky I felt I
was during the war. Lots of
people at home were far worse
off with the air raids and doo-
dle bugs in the cities and
towns. The way some people
used to sleep night after night in

Jack Weller taken at the back of the Bull Hotel

The White Horse and Maystons grocery shop, Ditchling

125

Above right: Our son Alan, now fifty,
tending his sheep

Above left: Our mentally handicapped
grandson, Mark

Left: Grand-daugther Rachel and
youngest great grand daughter

126

Myself and Anne with the great grand children

Andrew Stenning

the underground stations and shelters. The wonderful spirit that existed then, saw them through. It would be great if that spirit could return. "Lady Luck" certainly has played a great part during my lifetime. I thought the reference in my pay book was very fitting, signed by a Group Captain – "Whilst in the RAF LAc Stenning has done all that had been asked of him in a keen and efficient manner. He has proved himself a very keen and successful athlete. His technical knowledge gained in the Service should be of value in his civilian employment of farming." Ann and I are now in our fifty fifth year of marriage and I know how lucky I have been – again due to the war and our meeting at Gatwick.

John Stenning in the early 1980s

128